Counsels and Maxims

From The Essays Of Arthur Schopenhauer

Arthur Schopenhauer

Contents

COUNSELS AND MAXIMS
FROM THE ESSAYS OF ARTHUR

SCHOPENHAUER

BY

Arthur Schopenhauer

INTRODUCTION.

I f my object in these pages were to present a complete scheme of counsels and maxims for the guidance of life, I should have to repeat the numerous rules--some of them excellent--which have been drawn up by thinkers of all ages, from Theognis and Solomon[1] down to La Rochefoucauld; and, in so doing, I should inevitably entail upon the reader a vast amount of well-worn commonplace. But the fact is that in this work I make still less claim to exhaust my subject than in any other of my writings.

An author who makes no claims to completeness must also, in a great measure, abandon any attempt at systematic arrangement. For his double loss in this respect, the reader may console himself by reflecting that a complete and systematic treatment of such a subject as the guidance of life could hardly fail to be a very wearisome business. I have simply put down those of my thoughts which appear to be worth communicating--thoughts which, as far as I know, have not been uttered, or, at any rate, not just in the same form, by any one else; so that my remarks may be taken as a supplement to what has been already achieved in the immense field.

However, by way of introducing some sort of order into the great variety of matters upon which advice will be given in the following pages, I shall distribute what I have to say under the following heads: (1) general rules; (2) our relation to ourselves; (3) our relation to others; and finally, (4) rules which concern our manner of life and our worldly circumstances. I shall conclude with some remarks on the changes which the various periods of life produce in us.

---

1 I refer to the proverbs and maxims ascribed, in the Old Testament, to the king of that name.

CHAPTER I.
GENERAL RULES.--SECTION 1.

The first and foremost rule for the wise conduct of life seems to me to be contained in a view to which Aristotle parenthetically refers in the *Nichomachean Ethics*[2]: [Greek: o phronimoz to alupon dioke e ou to aedu] or, as it may be rendered, ***not pleasure, but freedom from pain, is what the wise man will aim at***.

The truth of this remark turns upon the negative character of happiness,--the fact that pleasure is only the negation of pain, and that pain is the positive element in life. Though I have given a detailed proof of this proposition in my chief work[3], I may supply one more illustration of it here, drawn from a circumstance of daily occurrence. Suppose that, with the exception of some sore or painful spot, we are physically in a sound and healthy condition: the sore of this one spot, will completely absorb our attention, causing us to lose the sense of general well-being, and destroying all our comfort in life. In the same way, when all our affairs but one turn out as we wish, the single instance in which our aims are frustrated is a constant trouble to us, even though it be something quite trivial. We think a great deal about it, and very little about those other and more important matters in which we have been successful. In both these cases what has met with resistance is ***the will***; in the one case, as it is objectified in the organism, in the other, as it presents itself in the struggle of life; and in both, it is plain that the satisfaction of the will consists in nothing else than that it meets with no resistance. It is, therefore, a satisfaction which is not directly felt; at most, we can become conscious of it only when we

---

2 vii. (12) 12.

3 ***Welt als Wille und Vorstellung***. Vol. I., p. 58.

reflect upon our condition. But that which checks or arrests the will is something positive; it proclaims its own presence. All pleasure consists in merely removing this check--in other words, in freeing us from its action; and hence pleasure is a state which can never last very long.

This is the true basis of the above excellent rule quoted from Aristotle, which bids us direct our aim, not toward securing what is pleasurable and agreeable in life, but toward avoiding, as far as possible, its innumerable evils. If this were not the right course to take, that saying of Voltaire's, ***Happiness is but a dream and sorrow is real***, would be as false as it is, in fact, true. A man who desires to make up the book of his life and determine where the balance of happiness lies, must put down in his accounts, not the pleasures which he has enjoyed, but the evils which he has escaped. That is the true method of eudaemonology; for all eudaemonology must begin by recognizing that its very name is a euphemism, and that ***to live happily*** only means ***to live less unhappily***--to live a tolerable life. There is no doubt that life is given us, not to be enjoyed, but to be overcome--to be got over. There are numerous expressions illustrating this--such as ***degere vitam, vita defungi***; or in Italian, ***si scampa cosi***; or in German, ***man muss suchen durchzukommen; er wird schon durch die Welt kommen***, and so on. In old age it is indeed a consolation to think that the work of life is over and done with. The happiest lot is not to have experienced the keenest delights or the greatest pleasures, but to have brought life to a close without any very great pain, bodily or mental. To measure the happiness of a life by its delights or pleasures, is to apply a false standard. For pleasures are and remain something negative; that they produce happiness is a delusion, cherished by envy to its own punishment. Pain is felt to be something positive, and hence its absence is the true standard of happiness. And if, over and above freedom from pain, there is also an absence of boredom, the essential conditions of earthly happiness are attained; for all else is chimerical.

It follows from this that a man should never try to purchase pleasure at the cost of pain, or even at the risk of incurring it; to do so is to pay what is positive and real, for what is negative and illusory; while there is a net profit in sacrificing pleasure for the sake of avoiding pain. In either case it is a matter of indifference whether the pain follows the pleasure or precedes it. While it is a complete inversion of the natural order to try and turn this scene of misery into a garden of pleasure, to aim at joy and pleasure rather than at the greatest possible freedom from pain--and yet how many do it!--there is some wisdom in taking a gloomy view, in looking upon the world as a kind of Hell, and in confining one's efforts to securing a little room that shall not be exposed to the fire. The fool rushes after the pleasures of life and finds himself their dupe; the wise man avoids its evils; and even if, notwithstanding his precautions, he falls into misfortunes, that is the fault of fate, not of his own folly. As far as he is successful in his endeavors, he cannot be said to have lived a life of illusion; for the evils which he shuns are very real. Even if he goes too far out of his way to avoid evils, and makes an unnecessary sacrifice of pleasure, he is, in reality, not the worse off for that; for all pleasures are chimerical, and to mourn for having lost any of them is a frivolous, and even ridiculous proceeding.

The failure to recognize this truth--a failure promoted by optimistic ideas--is the source of much unhappiness. In moments free from pain, our restless wishes present, as it were in a mirror, the image of a happiness that has no counterpart in reality, seducing us to follow it; in doing so we bring pain upon ourselves, and that is something undeniably real. Afterwards, we come to look with regret upon that lost state of painlessness; it is a paradise which we have gambled away; it is no longer with us, and we long in vain to undo what has been done.

One might well fancy that these visions of wishes fulfilled were the work of some evil spirit, conjured up in order to entice us away from that painless state which forms our highest happiness.

A careless youth may think that the world is meant to be enjoyed, as though it were the abode of some real or positive happiness, which only those fail to attain who are not clever enough to overcome the difficulties that lie in the way. This false notion takes a stronger hold on him when he comes to read poetry and romance, and to be deceived by outward show--the hypocrisy that characterizes the world from beginning to end; on which I shall have something to say presently. The result is that his life is the more or less deliberate pursuit of positive happiness; and happiness he takes to be equivalent to a series of definite pleasures. In seeking for these pleasures he encounters danger--a fact which should not be forgotten. He hunts for game that does not exist; and so he ends by suffering some very real and positive misfortune--pain, distress, sickness, loss, care, poverty, shame, and all the thousand ills of life. Too late he discovers the trick that has been played upon him.

But if the rule I have mentioned is observed, and a plan of life is adopted which proceeds by avoiding pain--in other words, by taking measures of precaution against want, sickness, and distress in all its forms, the aim is a real one, and something may be achieved which will be great in proportion as the plan is not disturbed by striving after the chimera of positive happiness. This agrees with the opinion expressed by Goethe in the *Elective Affinities*, and there put into the mouth of Mittler--the man who is always trying to make other people happy: *To desire to get rid of an evil is a definite object, but to desire a better fortune than one has is blind folly*. The same truth is contained in that fine French proverb: *le mieux est l'ennemi du bien*--leave well alone. And, as I have remarked in my chief work[4], this is the leading thought underlying the philosophical system of the Cynics. For what was it led the Cynics to repudiate pleasure in every form, if it was not the fact that pain is, in a greater or less degree, always bound up with pleasure? To go out of the way of pain seemed to them so much easier than to secure pleasure. Deeply impressed as they were by the negative nature of pleasure and the positive nature of pain, they consistently devoted all their efforts to the avoidance of pain. The first step to that end was, in their opinion, a complete and deliberate repudiation of pleasure, as something which served only to entrap the victim in order that he might be delivered over to pain.

We are all born, as Schiller says, in Arcadia. In other words, we come into the world full of claims to happiness and pleasure, and we cherish the fond hope of making them good. But, as a rule, Fate soon teaches us, in a rough and ready way that we really possess nothing at all, but that everything in the world is at its command, in virtue of an unassailable right, not only to all we have or acquire, to wife or child, but even to our very limbs, our arms, legs, *eyes* and ears, nay, even to the nose in the middle of our face. And in any case, after some little time, we learn by experience that happiness and pleasure are a *fata morgana*, which, visible from afar, vanish as we approach; that, on the other hand, suffering and pain are a reality, which makes its presence felt without any intermediary, and for its effect, stands in no need of illusion or the play of false hope.

If the teaching of experience bears fruit in us, we soon give up the pursuit of pleasure and happiness, and think much more about making ourselves secure against

4 *Welt als Wille und Vorstellung*, vol. ii., ch. 16.

the attacks of pain and suffering. We see that the best the world has to offer is an existence free from pain--a quiet, tolerable life; and we confine our claims to this, as to something we can more surely hope to achieve. For the safest way of not being very miserable is not to expect to be very happy. Merck, the friend of Goethe's youth, was conscious of this truth when he wrote: ***It is the wretched way people have of setting up a claim to happiness--and, that to, in a measure corresponding with their desires***--that ruins everything in this world. A man will make progress if he can get rid of this claim[5], and desire nothing but what he sees before him. Accordingly it is advisable to put very moderate limits upon our expectations of pleasure, possessions, rank, honor and so on; because it is just this striving and struggling to be happy, to dazzle the world, to lead a life full of pleasure, which entail great misfortune. It is prudent and wise, I say, to reduce one's claims, if only for the reason that it is extremely easy to be very unhappy; while to be very happy is not indeed difficult, but quite impossible. With justice sings the poet of life's wisdom:

> Auream quisquis mediocritatem
> Diligit, tutus caret obsoleti
> Sordibus tecti, caret invidenda
>   Sobrius aula.   Savius ventis agitatur ingens
> Pinus: et celsae graviori casu
> Decidunt turres; feriuntque summos
>   Fulgura monies[6].

--the golden mean is best--to live free from the squalor of a mean abode, and yet not be a mark for envy. It is the tall pine which is cruelly shaken by the wind, the highest summits that are struck in the storm, and the lofty towers that fall so heavily.

He who has taken to heart the teaching of my philosophy--who knows, therefore, that our whole existence is something which had better not have been, and that to disown and disclaim it is the highest wisdom--he will have no great expectations from anything or any condition in life: he will spend passion upon nothing

5   Letters to and from Merck.
6   Horace. Odes II. x.

in the world, nor lament over-much if he fails in any of his undertakings. He will feel the deep truth of what Plato[7] says: [Greek: oute ti ton anthropinon haxion on megalaes spondaes]--nothing in human affairs is worth any great anxiety; or, as the Persian poet has it,

> *Though from thy grasp all worldly things should flee,*
> *Grieve not for them, for they are nothing worth:*
> *And though a world in thy possession be,*
> *Joy not, for worthless are the things of earth.*
> *Since to that better world 'tis given to thee*
> *To pass, speed on, for this is nothing worth.*[8]

The chief obstacle to our arriving at these salutary views is that hypocrisy of the world to which I have already alluded--an hypocrisy which should be early revealed to the young. Most of the glories of the world are mere outward show, like the scenes on a stage: there is nothing real about them. Ships festooned and hung with pennants, firing of cannon, illuminations, beating of drums and blowing of trumpets, shouting and applauding--these are all the outward sign, the pretence and suggestion,--as it were the hieroglyphic,--of *joy*: but just there, joy is, as a rule, not to be found; it is the only guest who has declined to be present at the festival. Where this guest may really be found, he comes generally without invitation; he is not formerly announced, but slips in quietly by himself *sans facon*; often making his appearance under the most unimportant and trivial circumstances, and in the commonest company--anywhere, in short, but where the society is brilliant and distinguished. Joy is like the gold in the Australian mines--found only now and then, as it were, by the caprice of chance, and according to no rule or law; oftenest in very little grains, and very seldom in heaps. All that outward show which I have described, is only an attempt to make people believe that it is really joy which has

---

7 *Republic*, x. 604.

8 *Translator's Note*. From the Anvar-i Suhaili--*The Lights of Canopus*--being the Persian version of the *Table of Bidpai*. Translated by E.B. Eastwick, ch. iii. Story vi., p. 289.

come to the festival; and to produce this impression upon the spectators is, in fact, the whole object of it.

With ***mourning*** it is just the same. That long funeral procession, moving up so slowly; how melancholy it looks! what an endless row of carriages! But look into them--they are all empty; the coachmen of the whole town are the sole escort the dead man has to his grave. Eloquent picture of the friendship and esteem of the world! This is the falsehood, the hollowness, the hypocrisy of human affairs!

Take another example--a roomful of guests in full dress, being received with great ceremony. You could almost believe that this is a noble and distinguished company; but, as a matter of fact, it is compulsion, pain and boredom who are the real guests. For where many are invited, it is a rabble--even if they all wear stars. Really good society is everywhere of necessity very small. In brilliant festivals and noisy entertainments, there is always, at bottom, a sense of emptiness prevalent. A false tone is there: such gatherings are in strange contrast with the misery and barrenness of our existence. The contrast brings the true condition into greater relief. Still, these gatherings are effective from the outside; and that is just their purpose. Chamfort[9] makes the excellent remark that ***society--les cercles, les salons, ce qu'on appelle le monde***--is like a miserable play, or a bad opera, without any interest in itself, but supported for a time by mechanical aid, costumes and scenery.

And so, too, with academies and chairs of philosophy. You have a kind of signboard hung out to show the apparent abode of ***wisdom***: but wisdom is another guest who declines the invitation; she is to be found elsewhere. The chiming of bells, ecclesiastical millinery, attitudes of devotion, insane antics--these are the pretence, the false show of ***piety***. And so on. Everything in the world is like a hollow nut; there is little kernel anywhere, and when it does exist, it is still more rare to find it in the shell. You may look for it elsewhere, and find it, as a rule, only by chance.

SECTION 2. To estimate a man's condition in regard to happiness, it is necessary to ask, not what things please him, but what things trouble him; and the more

9 ***Translator's Note***. Nicholas "Chamfort" (1741-94), a French miscellaneous writer, whose brilliant conversation, power of sarcasm, and epigrammic force, coupled with an extraordinary career, render him one of the most interesting and remarkable men of his time. Schopenhauer undoubtedly owed much to this writer, to whom he constantly refers.

trivial these things are in themselves, the happier the man will be. To be irritated by trifles, a man must be well off; for in misfortunes trifles are unfelt.

SECTION 3. Care should be taken not to build the happiness of life upon a *broad foundation*--not to require a great many things in order to be happy. For happiness on such a foundation is the most easily undermined; it offers many more opportunities for accidents; and accidents are always happening. The architecture of happiness follows a plan in this respect just the opposite of that adopted in every other case, where the broadest foundation offers the greatest security. Accordingly, to reduce your claims to the lowest possible degree, in comparison with your means,--of whatever kind these may be--is the surest way of avoiding extreme misfortune.

To make extensive preparations for life--no matter what form they may take-- is one of the greatest and commonest of follies. Such preparations presuppose, in the first place, a long life, the full and complete term of years appointed to man--and how few reach it! and even if it be reached, it is still too short for all the plans that have been made; for to carry them out requites more time than was thought necessary at the beginning. And then how many mischances and obstacles stand in the way! how seldom the goal is ever reached in human affairs!

And lastly, even though the goal should be reached, the changes which Time works in us have been left out of the reckoning: we forget that the capacity whether for achievement or for enjoyment does not last a whole lifetime. So we often toil for things which are no longer suited to us when we attain them; and again, the years we spend in preparing for some work, unconsciously rob us of the power for carrying it out.

How often it happens that a man is unable to enjoy the wealth which he acquired at so much trouble and risk, and that the fruits of his labor are reserved for others; or that he is incapable of filling the position which he has won after so many years of toil and struggle. Fortune has come too late for him; or, contrarily, he has come too late for fortune,--when, for instance, he wants to achieve great things, say, in art or literature: the popular taste has changed, it may be; a new generation has grown up, which takes no interest in his work; others have gone a shorter way and got the start of him. These are the facts of life which Horace must have had in view, when he lamented the uselessness of all advice:--

> *quid eternis minorem*
> *Consiliis animum fatigas?*[10]

The cause of this commonest of all follies is that optical illusion of the mind from which everyone suffers, making life, at its beginning, seem of long duration; and at its end, when one looks back over the course of it, how short a time it seems! There is some advantage in the illusion; but for it, no great work would ever be done.

Our life is like a journey on which, as we advance, the landscape takes a different view from that which it presented at first, and changes again, as we come nearer. This is just what happens--especially with our wishes. We often find something else, nay, something better than what we are looking for; and what we look for, we often find on a very different path from that on which we began a vain search. Instead of finding, as we expected, pleasure, happiness, joy, we get experience, insight, knowledge--a real and permanent blessing, instead of a fleeting and illusory one.

This is the thought that runs through ***Wilkelm Meister***, like the bass in a piece of music. In this work of Goethe's, we have a novel of the ***intellectual*** kind, and, therefore, superior to all others, even to Sir Walter Scott's, which are, one and all, ***ethical***; in other words, they treat of human nature only from the side of the will. So, too, in the ***Zauberfloete***--that grotesque, but still significant, and even hieroglyphic--the same thought is symbolized, but in great, coarse lines, much in the way in which scenery is painted. Here the symbol would be complete if Tamino were in the end to be cured of his desire to possess Tainina, and received, in her stead, initiation into the mysteries of the Temple of Wisdom. It is quite right for Papageno, his necessary contrast, to succeed in getting his Papagena.

Men of any worth or value soon come to see that they are in the hands of Fate, and gratefully submit to be moulded by its teachings. They recognize that the fruit of life is experience, and not happiness; they become accustomed and content to exchange hope for insight; and, in the end, they can say, with Petrarch, that all they care for is to learn:--

---

10   Odes II. xi.

Altro diletto che 'mparar, non provo.

It may even be that they to some extent still follow their old wishes and aims, trifling with them, as it were, for the sake of appearances; all the while really and seriously looking for nothing but instruction; a process which lends them an air of genius, a trait of something contemplative and sublime.

In their search for gold, the alchemists discovered other things--gunpowder, china, medicines, the laws of nature. There is a sense in which we are all alchemists.

CHAPTER II.
OUR RELATION TO OURSELVES.--SECTION 4.

The mason employed on the building of a house may be quite ignorant of its general design; or at any rate, he may not keep it constantly in mind. So it is with man: in working through the days and hours of his life, he takes little thought of its character as a whole.

If there is any merit or importance attaching to a man's career, if he lays himself out carefully for some special work, it is all the more necessary and advisable for him to turn his attention now and then to its *plan*, that is to say, the miniature sketch of its general outlines. Of course, to do that, he must have applied the maxim [Greek: Gnothi seauton]; he must have made some little progress in the art of understanding himself. He must know what is his real, chief, and foremost object in life,--what it is that he most wants in order to be happy; and then, after that, what occupies the second and third place in his thoughts; he must find out what, on the whole, his vocation really is--the part he has to play, his general relation to the world. If he maps out important work for himself on great lines, a glance at this miniature plan of his life will, more than anything else stimulate, rouse and ennoble him, urge him on to action and keep him from false paths.

Again, just as the traveler, on reaching a height, gets a connected view over the road he has taken, with its many turns and windings; so it is only when we have completed a period in our life, or approach the end of it altogether, that we recognize the true connection between all our actions,--what it is we have achieved, what work we have done. It is only then that we see the precise chain of cause and effect, and the exact value of all our efforts. For as long as we are actually engaged in the work of life, we always act in accordance with the nature of our character, under the influence of motive, and within the limits of our capacity,--in a word, from beginning to end, under a law of ***necessity***; at every moment we do just what appears to us right and proper. It is only afterwards, when we come to look back at the whole course of our life and its general result, that we see the why and wherefore of it all.

When we are actually doing some great deed, or creating some immortal work, we are not conscious of it as such; we think only of satisfying present aims, of fulfilling the intentions we happen to have at the time, of doing the right thing at the moment. It is only when we come to view our life as a connected whole that our character and capacities show themselves in their true light; that we see how, in particular instances, some happy inspiration, as it were, led us to choose the only true path out of a thousand which might have brought us to ruin. It was our genius that guided us, a force felt in the affairs of the intellectual as in those of the world; and working by its defect just in the same way in regard to evil and disaster.

SECTION 5. Another important element in the wise conduct of life is to preserve a proper proportion between our thought for the present and our thought for the future; in order not to spoil the one by paying over-great attention to the other. Many live too long in the present--frivolous people, I mean; others, too much in the future, ever anxious and full of care. It is seldom that a man holds the right balance between the two extremes. Those who strive and hope and live only in the future, always looking ahead and impatiently anticipating what is coming, as something which will make them happy when they get it, are, in spite of their very clever airs, exactly like those donkeys one sees in Italy, whose pace may be hurried by fixing a stick on their heads with a wisp of hay at the end of it; this is always just in front of them, and they keep on trying to get it. Such people are in a constant state of illusion as to their whole existence; they go on living ***ad interim***, until at last they die.

Instead, therefore, of always thinking about our plans and anxiously looking to the future, or of giving ourselves up to regret for the past, we should never forget that the present is the only reality, the only certainty; that the future almost always turns out contrary to our expectations; that the past, too, was very different from what we suppose it to have been. But the past and the future are, on the whole, of less consequence than we think. Distance, which makes objects look small to the outward eye, makes them look big to the eye of thought. The present alone is true and actual; it is the only time which possesses full reality, and our existence lies in it exclusively. Therefore we should always be glad of it, and give it the welcome it deserves, and enjoy every hour that is bearable by its freedom from pain and annoyance with a full consciousness of its value. We shall hardly be able to do this if we make a wry face over the failure of our hopes in the past or over our anxiety for the future. It is the height of folly to refuse the present hour of happiness, or wantonly to spoil it by vexation at by-gones or uneasiness about what is to come. There is a time, of course, for forethought, nay, even for repentance; but when it is over let us think of what is past as of something to which we have said farewell, of necessity subduing our hearts--

> [Greek: alla ta men protuchthai easomen achnumenoi per
>   tumhon eni staethessi philon damasntes hanankae][11],

and of the future as of that which lies beyond our power, in the lap of the gods--

[Greek: all aetoi men tauta theon en gounasi keitai.][12]

But in regard to the present let us remember Seneca's advice, and live each day as if it were our whole life,--*singulas dies singulas vitas puta*: let us make it as agreeable as possible, it is the only real time we have.

Only those evils which are sure to come at a definite date have any right to disturb us; and how few there are which fulfill this description. For evils are of two kinds; either they are possible only, at most probable; or they are inevitable. Even in the case of evils which are sure to happen, the time at which they will happen is uncertain. A man who is always preparing for either class of evil will not have a moment of peace left him. So, if we are not to lose all comfort in life through the fear of evils, some of which are uncertain in themselves, and others, in the time at which they will occur, we should look upon the one kind as never likely to happen, and the other as not likely to happen very soon.

---

11 *Iliad*, xix, 65.
12 *Ibid*, xvii, 514

Now, the less our peace of mind is disturbed by fear, the more likely it is to be agitated by desire and expectation. This is the true meaning of that song of Goethe's which is such a favorite with everyone: *Ich hab' mein' Sach' auf nichts gestellt*. It is only after a man has got rid of all pretension, and taken refuge in mere unembellished existence, that he is able to attain that peace of mind which is the foundation of human happiness. Peace of mind! that is something essential to any enjoyment of the present moment; and unless its separate moments are enjoyed, there is an end of life's happiness as a whole. We should always collect that *To-day* comes only once, and never returns. We fancy that it will come again to-morrow; but *To-morrow* is another day, which, in its turn, comes once only. We are apt to forget that every day is an integral, and therefore irreplaceable portion of life, and to look upon life as though it were a collective idea or name which does not suffer if one of the individuals it covers is destroyed.

We should be more likely to appreciate and enjoy the present, if, in those good days when we are well and strong, we did not fail to reflect how, in sickness and sorrow, every past hour that was free from pain and privation seemed in our memory so infinitely to be envied--as it were, a lost paradise, or some one who was only then seen to have acted as a friend. But we live through our days of happiness without noticing them; it is only when evil comes upon us that we wish them back. A thousand gay and pleasant hours are wasted in ill-humor; we let them slip by unenjoyed, and sigh for them in vain when the sky is overcast. Those present moments that are bearable, be they never so trite and common,--passed by in indifference, or, it may be, impatiently pushed away,--those are the moments we should honor; never failing to remember that the ebbing tide is even how hurrying them into the past, where memory will store them transfigured and shining with an imperishable light,--in some after-time, and above all, when our days are evil, to raise the veil and present them as the object of our fondest regret.

SECTION 6. *Limitations always make for happiness*. We are happy in proportion as our range of vision, our sphere of work, our points of contact with the world, are restricted and circumscribed. We are more likely to feel worried and anxious if these limits are wide; for it means that our cares, desires and terrors are increased and intensified. That is why the blind are not so unhappy as we might be inclined to suppose; otherwise there would not be that gentle and almost serene expression of peace in their faces.

Another reason why limitation makes for happiness is that the second half of life proves even more dreary that the first. As the years wear on, the horizon of our aims and our points of contact with the world become more extended. In childhood our horizon is limited to the narrowest sphere about us; in youth there is already a very considerable widening of our view; in manhood it comprises the whole range of our activity, often stretching out over a very distant sphere,--the care, for instance, of a State or a nation; in old age it embraces posterity.

But even in the affairs of the intellect, limitation is necessary if we are to be happy. For the less the will is excited, the less we suffer. We have seen that suffering is something positive, and that happiness is only a negative condition. To limit the sphere of outward activity is to relieve the will of external stimulus: to limit the sphere of our intellectual efforts is to relieve the will of internal sources of excitement. This latter kind of limitation is attended by the disadvantage that it opens the door to boredom, which is a direct source of countless sufferings; for to banish boredom, a man will have recourse to any means that may be handy--dissipation, society, extravagance, gaming, and drinking, and the like, which in their turn bring mischief, ruin and misery in their train. ***Difficiles in otio quies***--it is difficult to keep quiet if you have nothing to do. That limitation in the sphere of outward activity is conducive, nay, even necessary to human happiness, such as it is, may be seen in the fact that the only kind of poetry which depicts men in a happy state of life--Idyllic poetry, I mean,--always aims, as an intrinsic part of its treatment, at representing them in very simple and restricted circumstances. It is this feeling, too, which is at the bottom of the pleasure we take in what are called ***genre*** pictures.

Simplicity, therefore, as far as it can be attained, and even ***monotony***, in our manner of life, if it does not mean that we are bored, will contribute to happiness; just because, under such circumstances, life, and consequently the burden which is the essential concomitant of life, will be least felt. Our existence will glide on peacefully like a stream which no waves or whirlpools disturb.

SECTION 7. Whether we are in a pleasant or a painful state depends, ultimately, upon the kind of matter that pervades and engrosses our consciousness. In this respect, purely intellectual occupation, for the mind that is capable of it, will, as a rule, do much more in the way of happiness than any form of practical life, with its constant alternations of success and failure, and all the shocks and torments it produces. But it must be confessed that for such occupation a pre-eminent amount of intellectual capacity is necessary. And in this connection it may be noted that, just as a life devoted to outward activity will distract and divert a man from study, and also deprive him of that quiet concentration of mind which is necessary for such work; so, on the other hand, a long course of thought will make him more or less unfit for the noisy pursuits of real life. It is advisable, therefore, to suspend mental work for a while, if circumstances happen which demand any degree of energy in affairs of a practical nature.

SECTION 8. To live a life that shall be entirely prudent and discreet, and to draw from experience all the instruction it contains, it is requisite to be constantly thinking back,--to make a kind of recapitulation of what we have done, of our impressions and sensations, to compare our former with our present judgments--what we set before us and struggle to achieve, with the actual result and satisfaction we have obtained. To do this is to get a repetition of the private lessons of experience,--lessons which are given to every one.

Experience of the world may be looked upon as a kind of text, to which reflection and knowledge form the commentary. Where there is great deal of reflection and intellectual knowledge, and very little experience, the result is like those books which have on each page two lines of text to forty lines of commentary. A great deal of experience with little reflection and scant knowledge, gives us books like those of the *editio Bipontina*[13] where there are no notes and much that is unintelligible.

The advice here given is on a par with a rule recommended by Pythagoras,--to review, every night before going to sleep, what we have done during the day. To live at random, in the hurly-burly of business or pleasure, without ever reflecting upon the past,--to go on, as it were, pulling cotton off the reel of life,--is to have no clear idea of what we are about; and a man who lives in this state will have chaos in his emotions and certain confusion in his thoughts; as is soon manifest by the abrupt and fragmentary character of his conversation, which becomes a kind of mincemeat. A man will be all the more exposed to this fate in proportion as he lives

---

13 *Translator's Note.* A series of Greek, Latin and French classics published at Zweibraecken in the Palatinate, from and after the year 1779. Cf. Butter, *Ueber die Bipontiner und die editiones Bipontinae*.

a restless life in the world, amid a crowd of various impressions and with a correspondingly small amount of activity on the part of his own mind.

And in this connection it will be in place to observe that, when events and circumstances which have influenced us pass away in the course of time, we are unable to bring back and renew the particular mood or state of feeling which they aroused in us: but we can remember what we were led to say and do in regard to them; and thus form, as it were, the result, expression and measure of those events. We should, therefore, be careful to preserve the memory of our thoughts at important points in our life; and herein lies the great advantage of keeping a journal.

SECTION 9. To be self-sufficient, to be all in all to oneself, to want for nothing, to be able to say **omnia mea mecum porto**--that is assuredly the chief qualification for happiness. Hence Aristotle's remark, [Greek: hae eudaimonia ton autarchon esti][14]--to be happy means to be self-sufficient--cannot be too often repeated. It is, at bottom, the same thought as is present in the very well-turned sentence from Chamfort:

Le bonheur n'est pas chose aisee: il est tres difficile de le trouver en nous, et impossible de le trouver ailleurs.

For while a man cannot reckon with certainty upon anyone but himself, the burdens and disadvantages, the dangers and annoyances, which arise from having to do with others, are not only countless but unavoidable.

There is no more mistaken path to happiness than worldliness, revelry, **high life**: for the whole object of it is to transform our miserable existence into a succession of joys, delights and pleasures,--a process which cannot fail to result in disappointment and delusion; on a par, in this respect, with its **obligato** accompaniment, the interchange of lies.[1]

[Footnote 1: As our body is concealed by the clothes we wear, so our mind is veiled in lies. The veil is always there, and it is only through it that we can sometimes guess at what a man really thinks; just as from his clothes we arrive at the general shape of his body.]

All society necessarily involves, as the first condition of its existence, mutual accommodation and restraint upon the part of its members. This means that the larger it is, the more insipid will be its tone. A man can be **himself** only so long as

14 *Eudem. Eth*. VII. ii. 37.

he is alone; and if he does not love solitude, he will not love freedom; for it is only when he is alone that he is really free. Constraint is always present in society, like a companion of whom there is no riddance; and in proportion to the greatness of a man's individuality, it will be hard for him to bear the sacrifices which all intercourse with others demands, Solitude will be welcomed or endured or avoided, according as a man's personal value is large or small,--the wretch feeling, when he is alone, the whole burden of his misery; the great intellect delighting in its greatness; and everyone, in short, being just what he is.

Further, if a man stands high in Nature's lists, it is natural and inevitable that he should feel solitary. It will be an advantage to him if his surroundings do not interfere with this feeling; for if he has to see a great deal of other people who are not of like character with himself, they will exercise a disturbing influence upon him, adverse to his peace of mind; they will rob him, in fact, of himself, and give him nothing to compensate for the loss.

But while Nature sets very wide differences between man and man in respect both of morality and of intellect, society disregards and effaces them; or, rather, it sets up artificial differences in their stead,--gradations of rank and position, which are very often diametrically opposed to those which Nature establishes. The result of this arrangement is to elevate those whom Nature has placed low, and to depress the few who stand high. These latter, then, usually withdraw from society, where, as soon as it is at all numerous, vulgarity reigns supreme.

What offends a great intellect in society is the equality of rights, leading to equality of pretensions, which everyone enjoys; while at the same time, inequality of capacity means a corresponding disparity of social power. So-called ***good society*** recognizes every kind of claim but that of intellect, which is a contraband article; and people are expected to exhibit an unlimited amount of patience towards every form of folly and stupidity, perversity and dullness; whilst personal merit has to beg pardon, as it were, for being present, or else conceal itself altogether. Intellectual superiority offends by its very existence, without any desire to do so.

The worst of what is called good society is not only that it offers us the companionship of people who are unable to win either our praise or our affection, but that it does not allow of our being that which we naturally are; it compels us, for the sake of harmony, to shrivel up, or even alter our shape altogether. Intellectual conversation, whether grave or humorous, is only fit for intellectual society; it is downright abhorrent to ordinary people, to please whom it is absolutely necessary to be commonplace and dull. This demands an act of severe self-denial; we have to forfeit three-fourths of ourselves in order to become like other people. No doubt their company may be set down against our loss in this respect; but the more a man is worth, the more he will find that what he gains does not cover what he loses, and that the balance is on the debit side of the account; for the people with whom he deals are generally bankrupt,--that is to say, there is nothing to be got from their society which can compensate either for its boredom, annoyance and disagreeableness, or for the self-denial which it renders necessary. Accordingly, most society is so constituted as to offer a good profit to anyone who will exchange it for solitude.

Nor is this all. By way of providing a substitute for real--I mean intellectual--superiority, which is seldom to be met with, and intolerable when it is found, society has capriciously adopted a false kind of superiority, conventional in its character, and resting upon arbitrary principles,--a tradition, as it were, handed down in the higher circles, and, like a password, subject to alteration; I refer to **bon-ton** fashion. Whenever this kind of superiority comes into collision with the real kind, its weakness is manifest. Moreover, the presence of **good tone** means the absence of **good sense**.

No man can be in **perfect accord** with any one but himself--not even with a friend or the partner of his life; differences of individuality and temperament are always bringing in some degree of discord, though it may be a very slight one. That genuine, profound peace of mind, that perfect tranquillity of soul, which, next to health, is the highest blessing the earth can give, is to be attained only in solitude, and, as a permanent mood, only in complete retirement; and then, if there is anything great and rich in the man's own self, his way of life is the happiest that may be found in this wretched world.

Let me speak plainly. However close the bond of friendship, love, marriage--a man, ultimately, looks to himself, to his own welfare alone; at most, to his child's too. The less necessity there is for you to come into contact with mankind in general, in the relations whether of business or of personal intimacy, the better off you are. Loneliness and solitude have their evils, it is true; but if you cannot feel them all at once, you can at least see where they lie; on the other hand, society is **insidi-**

ous in this respect; as in offering you what appears to be the pastime of pleasing social intercourse, it works great and often irreparable mischief. The young should early be trained to bear being left alone; for it is a source of happiness and peace of mind.

It follows from this that a man is best off if he be thrown upon his own resources and can be all in all to himself; and Cicero goes so far as to say that a man who is in this condition cannot fail to be very happy--*nemo potest non beatissimus esse qui est totus aptus ex sese, quique in se uno ponit omnia*[15]. The more a man has in himself, the less others can be to him. The feeling of self-sufficiency! it is that which restrains those whose personal value is in itself great riches, from such considerable sacrifices as are demanded by intercourse with the world, let alone, then, from actually practicing self-denial by going out of their way to seek it. Ordinary people are sociable and complaisant just from the very opposite feeling;--to bear others' company is easier for them than to bear their own. Moreover, respect is not paid in this world to that which has real merit; it is reserved for that which has none. So retirement is at once a proof and a result of being distinguished by the possession of meritorious qualities. It will therefore show real wisdom on the part of any one who is worth anything in himself, to limit his requirements as may be necessary, in order to preserve or extend his freedom, and,--since a man must come into some relations with his fellow-men--to admit them to his intimacy as little as possible.

I have said that people are rendered sociable by their ability to endure solitude, that is to say, their own society. They become sick of themselves. It is this vacuity of soul which drives them to intercourse with others,--to travels in foreign countries. Their mind is wanting in elasticity; it has no movement of its own, and so they try to give it some,--by drink, for instance. How much drunkenness is due to this cause alone! They are always looking for some form of excitement, of the strongest kind they can bear--the excitement of being with people of like nature with themselves; and if they fail in this, their mind sinks by its own weight, and they fall into a grievous lethargy[16]. Such people, it may be said, possess only a small fraction of humanity

---

15 *Paradoxa Stoidorum*: II.

16 It is a well-known fact, that we can more easily bear up under evils which fall upon a great many people besides ourselves. As boredom seems to be an evil of this kind, people band together to offer it a common resistance. The love of life is

in themselves; and it requires a great many of them put together to make up a fair amount of it,--to attain any degree of consciousness as men. A man, in the full sense of the word,--a man *par excellence*--does not represent a fraction, but a whole number: he is complete in himself.

Ordinary society is, in this respect, very like the kind of music to be obtained from an orchestra composed of Russian horns. Each horn has only one note; and the music is produced by each note coming in just at the right moment. In the monotonous sound of a single horn, you have a precise illustration of the effect of most people's minds. How often there seems to be only one thought there! and no room for any other. It is easy to see why people are so bored; and also why they are sociable, why they like to go about in crowds--why mankind is so *gregarious*. It is the monotony of his own nature that makes a man find solitude intolerable. *Omnis stultitia laborat fastidio sui*: folly is truly its own burden. Put a great many men together, and you may get some result--some music from your horns!

A man of intellect is like an artist who gives a concert without any help from anyone else, playing on a single instrument--a piano, say, which is a little orchestra in itself. Such a man is a little world in himself; and the effect produced by various instruments together, he produces single-handed, in the unity of his own consciousness. Like the piano, he has no place in a symphony: he is a soloist and performs by himself,--in solitude, it may be; or, if in company with other instruments, only as principal; or for setting the tone, as in singing. However, those who

---

at bottom only the fear of death; and, in the same way, the social impulse does not rest directly upon the love of society, but upon the fear of solitude; it is not alone the charm of being in others' company that people seek, it is the dreary oppression of being alone--the monotony of their own consciousness--that they would avoid. They will do anything to escape it,--even tolerate bad companions, and put up with the feeling of constraint which all society involves, in this case a very burdensome one. But if aversion to such society conquers the aversion to being alone, they become accustomed to solitude and hardened to its immediate effects. They no longer find solitude to be such a very bad thing, and settle down comfortably to it without any hankering after society;--and this, partly because it is only indirectly that they need others' company, and partly because they have become accustomed to the benefits of being alone.

are fond of society from time to time may profit by this simile, and lay it down as a general rule that deficiency of quality in those we meet may be to some extent compensated by an increase in quantity. One man's company may be quite enough, if he is clever; but where you have only ordinary people to deal with, it is advisable to have a great many of them, so that some advantage may accrue by letting them all work together,--on the analogy of the horns; and may Heaven grant you patience for your task!

That mental vacuity and barrenness of soul to which I have alluded, is responsible for another misfortune. When men of the better class form a society for promoting some noble or ideal aim, the result almost always is that the innumerable mob of humanity comes crowding in too, as it always does everywhere, like vermin--their object being to try and get rid of boredom, or some other defect of their nature; and anything that will effect that, they seize upon at once, without the slightest discrimination. Some of them will slip into that society, or push themselves in, and then either soon destroy it altogether, or alter it so much that in the end it comes to have a purpose the exact opposite of that which it had at first.

This is not the only point of view from which the social impulse may be regarded. On cold days people manage to get some warmth by crowding together; and you can warm your mind in the same way--by bringing it into contact with others. But a man who has a great deal of intellectual warmth in himself will stand in no need of such resources. I have written a little fable illustrating this: it may be found elsewhere[17]. As a general rule, it may be said that a man's sociability stands

---

17 *Translator's Note*. The passage to which Schopenhauer refers is *Parerga*: vol. ii. Sec. 413 (4th edition). The fable is of certain porcupines, who huddled together for warmth on a cold day; but as they began to prick one another with their quills, they were obliged to disperse. However the cold drove them together again, when just the same thing happened. At last, after many turns of huddling and dispersing, they discovered that they would be best off by remaining at a little distance from one another. In the same way, the need of society drives the human porcupines together--only to be mutually repelled by the many prickly and disagreeable qualities of their nature. The moderate distance which they at last discover to be the only tolerable condition of intercourse, is the code of politeness and fine manners; and those who transgress it are roughly told--in the English phrase--*to keep their*

very nearly in inverse ratio to his intellectual value: to say that "so and so" is very unsociable, is almost tantamount to saying that he is a man of great capacity.

Solitude is doubly advantageous to such a man. Firstly, it allows him to be with himself, and, secondly, it prevents him being with others--an advantage of great moment; for how much constraint, annoyance, and even danger there is in all intercourse with the world. *Tout notre mal*, says La Bruyere, *vient de ne pouvoir etre seul*. It is really a very risky, nay, a fatal thing, to be sociable; because it means contact with natures, the great majority of which are bad morally, and dull or perverse, intellectually. To be unsociable is not to care about such people; and to have enough in oneself to dispense with the necessity of their company is a great piece of good fortune; because almost all our sufferings spring from having to do with other people; and that destroys the peace of mind, which, as I have said, comes next after health in the elements of happiness. Peace of mind is impossible without a considerable amount of solitude. The Cynics renounced all private property in order to attain the bliss of having nothing to trouble them; and to renounce society with the same object is the wisest thing a man can do. Bernardin de Saint Pierre has the very excellent and pertinent remark that to be sparing in regard to food is a means of health; in regard to society, a means of tranquillity--*la diete des ailmens nous rend la sante du corps, et celle des hommes la tranquillite de l'ame.* To be soon on friendly, or even affectionate, terms with solitude is like winning a gold mine; but this is not something which everybody can do. The prime reason for social intercourse is mutual need; and as soon as that is satisfied, boredom drives people together once more. If it were not for these two reasons, a man would probably elect to remain alone; if only because solitude is the sole condition of life which gives full play to that feeling of exclusive importance which every man has in his own eyes,-- as if he were the only person in the world! a feeling which, in the throng and press of real life, soon shrivels up to nothing, getting, at every step, a painful *dementi*. From this point of view it may be said that solitude is the original and natural state of man, where, like another Adam, he is as happy as his nature will allow.

distance. By this arrangement the mutual need of warmth is only very moderately satisfied,--but then people do not get pricked. A man who has some heat in himself prefers to remain outside, where he will neither prick other people nor get pricked himself.

But still, had Adam no father or mother? There is another sense in which solitude is not the natural state; for, at his entrance into the world, a man finds himself with parents, brothers, sisters, that is to say, in society, and not alone. Accordingly it cannot be said that the love of solitude is an original characteristic of human nature; it is rather the result of experience and reflection, and these in their turn depend upon the development of intellectual power, and increase with the years.

Speaking generally, sociability stands in inverse ratio with age. A little child raises a piteous cry of fright if it is left alone for only a few minutes; and later on, to be shut up by itself is a great punishment. Young people soon get on very friendly terms with one another; it is only the few among them of any nobility of mind who are glad now and then to be alone;--but to spend the whole day thus would be disagreeable. A grown-up man can easily do it; it is little trouble to him to be much alone, and it becomes less and less trouble as he advances in years. An old man who has outlived all his friends, and is either indifferent or dead to the pleasures of life, is in his proper element in solitude; and in individual cases the special tendency to retirement and seclusion will always be in direct proportion to intellectual capacity.

For this tendency is not, as I have said, a purely natural one; it does not come into existence as a direct need of human nature; it is rather the effect of the experience we go through, the product of reflection upon what our needs really are; proceeding, more especially, from the insight we attain into the wretched stuff of which most people are made, whether you look at their morals or their intellects. The worst of it all is that, in the individual, moral and intellectual shortcomings are closely connected and play into each other's hands, so that all manner of disagreeable results are obtained, which make intercourse with most people not only unpleasant but intolerable. Hence, though the world contains many things which are thoroughly bad, the worst thing in it is society. Even Voltaire, that sociable Frenchman, was obliged to admit that there are everywhere crowds of people not worth talking to: *la terre est couverte de gens qui ne meritent pas qu'on leur parle*. And Petrarch gives a similar reason for wishing to be alone--that tender spirit! so strong and constant in his love of seclusion. The streams, the plains and woods know well, he says, how he has tried to escape the perverse and stupid people who have missed the way to heaven:--

Cercato ho sempre solitaria vita
  (Le rive il sanno, e le campagne e i boschi)
Per fuggir quest' ingegni storti e loschi
  Che la strada del ciel' hanno smarrita.

He pursues the same strain in that delightful book of his, *DeVita Solitaria*, which seems to have given Zimmerman the idea of his celebrated work on *Solitude*. It is the secondary and indirect character of the love of seclusion to which Chamfort alludes in the following passage, couched in his sarcastic vein: *On dit quelquefois d'un homme qui vit seul, il n'aime pas la societe. C'est souvent comme si on disait d'un homme qu'il n'aime pas la promenade, sous le pretexte qu'il ne se promene pas volontiers le soir dans le foret de Bondy.*

You will find a similar sentiment expressed by the Persian poet Sadi, in his *Garden of Roses. Since that time*, he says, *we have taken leave of society, preferring the path of seclusion; for there is safety in solitude*. Angelus Silesius[18], a very gentle and Christian writer, confesses to the same feeling, in his own mythical language. Herod, he says, is the common enemy; and when, as with Joseph, God warns us of danger, we fly from the world to solitude, from Bethlehem to Egypt; or else suffering and death await us!--

    Herodes ist ein Feind; der Joseph der Verstand,   Dem machte Gott die Gefahr im Traum (in Geist) bekannt; Die Welt ist Bethlehem, Aegypten Einsamkeit, Fleuch, meine Seele! fleuch, sonst stirbest du vor Leid.

Giordano Bruno also declares himself a friend of seclusion. *Tanti uomini*, he says, *che in terra hanno voluto gustare vita celeste, dissero con una voce, "ecce elongavi fugiens et mansi in solitudine"*--those who in this world have desired a foretaste of the divine life, have always proclaimed with one voice:

  Lo! then would I wander far off; I would lodge in the wilderness[19].

And in the work from which I have already quoted, Sadi says of himself: ***In disgust with my friends at Damascus, I withdrew into the desert about Jerusa-***

18 *Translator's Note*. Angelus Silesius, pseudonym for Johannes Scheffler, a physician and mystic poet of the seventeenth century (1624-77).
19 Psalms, lv. 7.

lem, to seek the society of the beasts of the field. In short, the same thing has been said by all whom Prometheus has formed out of better clay. What pleasure could they find in the company of people with whom their only common ground is just what is lowest and least noble in their own nature--the part of them that is commonplace, trivial and vulgar? What do they want with people who cannot rise to a higher level, and for whom nothing remains but to drag others down to theirs? for this is what they aim at. It is an aristocratic feeling that is at the bottom of this propensity to seclusion and solitude.

Rascals are always sociable--more's the pity! and the chief sign that a man has any nobility in his character is the little pleasure he takes in others' company. He prefers solitude more and more, and, in course of time, comes to see that, with few exceptions, the world offers no choice beyond solitude on one side and vulgarity on the other. This may sound a hard thing to say; but even Angelus Silesius, with all his Christian feelings of gentleness and love, was obliged to admit the truth of it. However painful solitude may be, he says, be careful not to be vulgar; for then you may find a desert everywhere:--

> *Die Einsamkeit ist noth: doch sei nur nicht gemein,*
> *So kannst du ueberall in einer Wueste sein*.

It is natural for great minds--the true teachers of humanity--to care little about the constant company of others; just as little as the schoolmaster cares for joining in the gambols of the noisy crowd of boys which surround him. The mission of these great minds is to guide mankind over the sea of error to the haven of truth--to draw it forth from the dark abysses of a barbarous vulgarity up into the light of culture and refinement. Men of great intellect live in the world without really belonging to it; and so, from their earliest years, they feel that there is a perceptible difference between them and other people. But it is only gradually, with the lapse of years, that they come to a clear understanding of their position. Their intellectual isolation is then reinforced by actual seclusion in their manner of life; they let no one approach who is not in some degree emancipated from the prevailing vulgarity.

From what has been said it is obvious that the love of solitude is not a direct, original impulse in human nature, but rather something secondary and of gradual growth. It is the more distinguishing feature of nobler minds, developed not without some conquest of natural desires, and now and then in actual opposition to the promptings of Mephistopheles--bidding you exchange a morose and soul-destroying solitude for life amongst men, for society; even the worst, he says, will give a sense of human fellowship:--

> Hoer' auf mit deinem Gram zu spielen,
> Der, wie ein Geier, dir am Leben frisst:
> Die schlechteste Gesellschaft laesst dich fuehlen
> Dass du ein Mensch mit Menschen bist[20].

To be alone is the fate of all great minds--a fate deplored at times, but still always chosen as the less grievous of two evils. As the years increase, it always becomes easier to say, Dare to be wise--*sapere aude*. And after sixty, the inclination to be alone grows into a kind of real, natural instinct; for at that age everything combines in favor of it. The strongest impulse--the love of woman's society--has little or no effect; it is the sexless condition of old age which lays the foundation of a certain self-sufficiency, and that gradually absorbs all desire for others' company. A thousand illusions and follies are overcome; the active years of life are in most cases gone; a man has no more expectations or plans or intentions. The generation to which he belonged has passed away, and a new race has sprung up which looks upon him as essentially outside its sphere of activity. And then the years pass more quickly as we become older, and we want to devote our remaining time to the intellectual rather than to the practical side of life. For, provided that the mind retains its faculties, the amount of knowledge and experience we have acquired, together with the facility we have gained in the use of our powers, makes it then more than ever easy and interesting to us to pursue the study of any subject. A thousand things become clear which were formerly enveloped in obscurity, and results are obtained which give a feeling of difficulties overcome. From long experience of men, we cease to expect much from them; we find that, on the whole, people do not gain by a nearer acquaintance; and that--apart from a few rare and fortunate exceptions--we have come across none but defective specimens of human nature which it is

---

20 Goethe's *Faust*, Part I., 1281-5.

advisable to leave in peace. We are no more subject to the ordinary illusions of life; and as, in individual instances, we soon see what a man is made of, we seldom feel any inclination to come into closer relations with him. Finally, isolation--our own society--has become a habit, as it were a second nature to us, more especially if we have been on friendly terms with it from our youth up. The love of solitude which was formerly indulged only at the expense of our desire for society, has now come to be the simple quality of our natural disposition--the element proper to our life, as water to a fish. This is why anyone who possesses a unique individuality--unlike others and therefore necessarily isolated--feels that, as he becomes older, his position is no longer so burdensome as when he was young.

For, as a matter of fact, this very genuine privilege of old age is one which can be enjoyed only if a man is possessed of a certain amount of intellect; it will be appreciated most of all where there is real mental power; but in some degree by every one. It is only people of very barren and vulgar nature who will be just as sociable in their old age as they were in their youth. But then they become troublesome to a society to which they are no longer suited, and, at most, manage to be tolerated; whereas, they were formerly in great request.

There is another aspect of this inverse proportion between age and sociability--the way in which it conduces to education. The younger that people are, the more in every respect they have to learn; and it is just in youth that Nature provides a system of mutual education, so that mere intercourse with others, at that time of life, carries instruction with it. Human society, from this point of view, resembles a huge academy of learning, on the Bell and Lancaster system, opposed to the system of education by means of books and schools, as something artificial and contrary to the institutions of Nature. It is therefore a very suitable arrangement that, in his young days, a man should be a very diligent student at the place of learning provided by Nature herself.

But there is nothing in life which has not some drawback--*nihil est ab omni parte beatum*, as Horace says; or, in the words of an Indian proverb, *no lotus without a stalk*. Seclusion, which has so many advantages, has also its little annoyances and drawbacks, which are small, however, in comparison with those of society; hence anyone who is worth much in himself will get on better without other people than with them. But amongst the disadvantages of seclusion there is one which is not so easy to see as the rest. It is this: when people remain indoors all day, they become physically very sensitive to atmospheric changes, so that every little draught is enough to make them ill; so with our temper; a long course of seclusion makes it so sensitive that the most trivial incidents, words, or even looks, are sufficient to disturb or to vex and offend us--little things which are unnoticed by those who live in the turmoil of life.

When you find human society disagreeable and feel yourself justified in flying to solitude, you can be so constituted as to be unable to bear the depression of it for any length of time, which will probably be the case if you are young. Let me advise you, then, to form the habit of taking some of your solitude with you into society, to learn to be to some extent alone even though you are in company; not to say at once what you think, and, on the other hand, not to attach too precise a meaning to what others say; rather, not to expect much of them, either morally or intellectually, and to strengthen yourself in the feeling of indifference to their opinion, which is the surest way of always practicing a praiseworthy toleration. If you do that, you will not live so much with other people, though you may appear to move amongst them: your relation to them will be of a purely objective character. This precaution will keep you from too close contact with society, and therefore secure you against being contaminated or even outraged by it[21]. Society is in this respect like a fire--the wise man warming himself at a proper distance from it; not coming too close, like the fool, who, on getting scorched, runs away and shivers in solitude, loud in his complaint that the fire burns.

SECTION 10. *Envy* is natural to man; and still, it is at once a vice and a source of misery[22]. We should treat it as the enemy of our happiness, and stifle it like an evil thought. This is the advice given by Seneca; as he well puts it, we shall be pleased with what we have, if we avoid the self-torture of comparing our own lot with some other and happier one--nostra nos sine comparatione delectent; nunquam

---

21   This restricted, or, as it were, entrenched kind of sociability has been dramatically illustrated in a play--well worth reading--of Moratin's, entitled ***El Cafe o sea la Comedia Nuova*** (The Cafe or the New Comedy), chiefly by one of the characters, Don Pedro and especially in the second and third scenes of the first act.

22   Envy shows how unhappy people are; and their constant attention to what others do and leave undone, how much they are bored.

erit felix quem torquebit felicior[23]. ***And again,*** quum adspexeris quot te antecedent, cogita quot sequantur[24]--if a great many people appear to be better off than yourself, think how many there are in a worse position. It is a fact that if real calamity comes upon us, the most effective consolation--though it springs from the same source as envy--is just the thought of greater misfortunes than ours; and the next best is the society of those who are in the same luck as we--the partners of our sorrows.

So much for the envy which we may feel towards others. As regards the envy which we may excite in them, it should always be remembered that no form of hatred is so implacable as the hatred that comes from envy; and therefore we should always carefully refrain from doing anything to rouse it; nay, as with many another form of vice, it is better altogether to renounce any pleasure there may be in it, because of the serious nature of its consequences.

Aristocracies are of three kinds: (1) of birth and rank; (2) of wealth; and (3) of intellect. The last is really the most distinguished of the three, and its claim to occupy the first position comes to be recognized, if it is only allowed time to work. So eminent a king as Frederick the Great admitted it--***les ames privilegiees rangent a l'egal des souverains***, as he said to his chamberlain, when the latter expressed his surprise that Voltaire should have a seat at the table reserved for kings and princes, whilst ministers and generals were relegated to the chamberlain's.

Every one of these aristocracies is surrounded by a host of envious persons. If you belong to one of them, they will be secretly embittered against you; and unless they are restrained by fear, they will always be anxious to let you understand that ***you are no better than they***. It is by their anxiety to let you know this, that they betray how greatly they are conscious that the opposite is the truth.

The line of conduct to be pursued if you are exposed to envy, is to keep the envious persons at a distance, and, as far as possible, avoid all contact with them, so that there may be a wide gulf fixed between you and them; if this cannot be done, to bear their attacks with the greatest composure. In the latter case, the very thing that provokes the attack will also neutralize it. This is what appears to be generally done.

The members of one of these aristocracies usually get on very well with those

---

23   ***De Ira***: iii., 30.
24   Epist. xv.

of another, and there is no call for envy between them, because their several privileges effect an equipoise.

SECTION 11. Give mature and repeated consideration to any plan before you proceed to carry it out; and even after you have thoroughly turned it over in your mind, make some concession to the incompetency of human judgment; for it may always happen that circumstances which cannot be investigated or foreseen, will come in and upset the whole of your calculation. This is a reflection that will always influence the negative side of the balance--a kind of warning to refrain from unnecessary action in matters of importance--*quieta non movere.* But having once made up your mind and begun your work, you must let it run its course and abide the result--not worry yourself by fresh reflections on what is already accomplished, or by a renewal of your scruples on the score of possible danger: free your mind from the subject altogether, and refuse to go into it again, secure in the thought that you gave it mature attention at the proper time. This is the same advice as is given by an Italian proverb--*legala bene e poi lascia la andare*--which Goethe has translated thus: See well to your girths, and then ride on boldly[25].

And if, notwithstanding that, you fail, it is because human affairs are the sport of chance and error. Socrates, the wisest of men, needed the warning voice of his good genius, or [Greek: daimonion], to enable him to do what was right in regard to his own personal affairs, or at any rate, to avoid mistakes; which argues that the human intellect is incompetent for the purpose. There is a saying--which is reported to have originated with one of the Popes--that when misfortune happens to us, the blame of it, at least in some degree, attaches to ourselves. If this is not true absolutely and in every instance, it is certainly true in the great majority of cases. It even looks as if this truth had a great deal to do with the effort people make as far as possible to conceal their misfortunes, and to put the best face they can upon them, for fear lest their misfortunes may show how much they are to blame.

SECTION 12.

In the case of a misfortune which has already happened and therefore cannot be altered, you should not allow yourself to think that it might have been otherwise; still less, that it might have been avoided by such and such means; for reflec-

---

25   It may be observed, in passing, that a great many of the maxims which Goethe puts under the head of *Proverbial*, are translations from the Italian.

tions of this kind will only add to your distress and make it intolerable, so that you will become a tormentor to yourself--[Greek: heautontimoroumeaeos]. It is better to follow the example of King David; who, as long as his son lay on the bed of sickness, assailed Jehovah with unceasing supplications and entreaties for his recovery; but when he was dead, snapped his fingers and thought no more of it. If you are not light-hearted enough for that, you can take refuge in fatalism, and have the great truth revealed to you that everything which happens is the result of necessity, and therefore inevitable.

However good this advice may be, it is one-sided and partial. In relieving and quieting us for the moment, it is no doubt effective enough; but when our misfortunes have resulted--as is usually the case--from our own carelessness or folly, or, at any rate, partly by our own fault, it is a good thing to consider how they might have been avoided, and to consider it often in spite of its being a tender subject--a salutary form of self-discipline, which will make us wiser and better men for the future. If we have made obvious mistakes, we should not try, as we generally do, to gloss them over, or to find something to excuse or extenuate them; we should admit to ourselves that we have committed faults, and open our eyes wide to all their enormity, in order that we may firmly resolve to avoid them in time to come. To be sure, that means a great deal of self-inflicted pain, in the shape of discontent, but it should be remembered that to spare the rod is to spoil the child--[Greek: ho mae dareis anthropos ou paideuetai][26].

SECTION 13. In all matters affecting our weal or woe, we should be careful not to let our imagination run away with us, and build no castles in the air. In the first place, they are expensive to build, because we have to pull them down again immediately, and that is a source of grief. We should be still more on our guard against distressing our hearts by depicting possible misfortunes. If these were misfortunes of a purely imaginary kind, or very remote and unlikely, we should at once see, on awaking from our dream, that the whole thing was mere illusion; we should rejoice all the more in a reality better than our dreams, or at most, be warned against misfortunes which, though very remote, were still possible. These, however, are not the sort of playthings in which imagination delights; it is only in idle hours that we build castles in the air, and they are always of a pleasing description. The mat-

---

26 Menander. Monost: 422.

ter which goes to form gloomy dreams are mischances which to some extent really threaten us, though it be from some distance; imagination makes us look larger and nearer and more terrible than they are in reality. This is a kind of dream which cannot be so readily shaken off on awaking as a pleasant one; for a pleasant dream is soon dispelled by reality, leaving, at most, a feeble hope lying in the lap of possibility. Once we have abandoned ourselves to a fit of the blues, visions are conjured up which do not so easily vanish again; for it is always just possible that the visions may be realized. But we are not always able to estimate the exact degree of possibility: possibility may easily pass into probability; and thus we deliver ourselves up to torture. Therefore we should be careful not to be over-anxious on any matter affecting our weal or our woe, not to carry our anxiety to unreasonable or injudicious limits; but coolly and dispassionately to deliberate upon the matter, as though it were an abstract question which did not touch us in particular. We should give no play to imagination here; for imagination is not judgment--it only conjures up visions, inducing an unprofitable and often very painful mood.

The rule on which I am here insisting should be most carefully observed towards evening. For as darkness makes us timid and apt to see terrifying shapes everywhere, there is something similar in the effect of indistinct thought; and uncertainty always brings with it a sense of danger. Hence, towards evening, when our powers of thought and judgment are relaxed,--at the hour, as it were, of subjective darkness,--the intellect becomes tired, easily confused, and unable to get at the bottom of things; and if, in that state, we meditate on matters of personal interest to ourselves, they soon assume a dangerous and terrifying aspect. This is mostly the case at night, when we are in bed; for then the mind is fully relaxed, and the power of judgment quite unequal to its duties; but imagination is still awake. Night gives a black look to everything, whatever it may be. This is why our thoughts, just before we go to sleep, or as we lie awake through the hours of the night, are usually such confusions and perversions of facts as dreams themselves; and when our thoughts at that time are concentrated upon our own concerns, they are generally as black and monstrous as possible. In the morning all such nightmares vanish like dreams: as the Spanish proverb has it, ***noche tinta, bianco el dia***--the night is colored, the day is white. But even towards nightfall, as soon as the candles are lit, the mind, like the eye, no longer sees things so clearly as by day: it is a time unsuited to serious meditation, especially on unpleasant subjects. The morning is the proper time for that--as indeed for all efforts without exception, whether mental or bodily. For the morning is the youth of the day, when everything is bright, fresh, and easy of attainment; we feel strong then, and all our faculties are completely at our disposal. Do not shorten the morning by getting up late, or waste it in unworthy occupations or in talk; look upon it as the quintessence of life, as to a certain extent sacred. Evening is like old age: we are languid, talkative, silly. Each day is a little life: every waking and rising a little birth, every fresh morning a little youth, every going to rest and sleep a little death.

But condition of health, sleep, nourishment, temperature, weather, surroundings, and much else that is purely external, have, in general, an important influence upon our mood and therefore upon our thoughts. Hence both our view of any matter and our capacity for any work are very much subject to time and place. So it is best to profit by a good mood--for how seldom it comes!--

> *Nehmt die gute Stimmung wahr,*
> *Denn sie kommt so selten*[27].

We are not always able to form new ideas about; our surroundings, or to command original thoughts: they come if they will, and when they will. And so, too, we cannot always succeed in completely considering some personal matter at the precise time at which we have determined beforehand to consider it, and just when we set ourselves to do so. For the peculiar train of thought which is favorable to it may suddenly become active without any special call being made upon it, and we may then follow it up with keen interest. In this way reflection, too, chooses its own time.

This reining-in of the imagination which I am recommending, will also forbid us to summon up the memory of the past misfortune, to paint a dark picture of the injustice or harm that has been done us, the losses we have sustained, the insults, slights and annoyances to which we have been exposed: for to do that is to rouse into fresh life all those hateful passions long laid asleep--the anger and resentment which disturb and pollute our nature. In an excellent parable, Proclus, the Neopla-

---

27 Goethe.

tonist, points out how in every town the mob dwells side by side with those who are rich and distinguished: so, too, in every man, be he never so noble and dignified, there is, in the depth of his nature, a mob of low and vulgar desires which constitute him an animal. It will not do to let this mob revolt or even so much as peep forth from its hiding-place; it is hideous of mien, and its rebel leaders are those flights of imagination which I have been describing. The smallest annoyance, whether it comes from our fellow-men or from the things around us, may swell up into a monster of dreadful aspect, putting us at our wits' end--and all because we go on brooding over our troubles and painting them in the most glaring colors and on the largest scale. It is much better to take a very calm and prosaic view of what is disagreeable; for that is the easiest way of bearing it.

If you hold small objects close to your eyes, you limit your field of vision and shut out the world. And, in the same way, the people or the things which stand nearest, even though they are of the very smallest consequence, are apt to claim an amount of attention much beyond their due, occupying us disagreeably, and leaving no room for serious thoughts and affairs of importance. We ought to work against this tendency.

SECTION 14. The sight of things which do not belong to us is very apt to raise the thought: *Ah, if that were only mine*! making us sensible of our privation. Instead of that we should do better by more frequently putting to ourselves the opposite case: *Ah, if that were not mine*. What I mean is that we should sometimes try to look upon our possessions in the light in which they would appear if we had lost them; whatever they may be, property, health, friends, a wife or child or someone else we love, our horse or our dog--it is usually only when we have lost them that we begin to find out their value. But if we come to look at things in the way I recommend, we shall be doubly the gainers; we shall at once get more pleasure out of them than we did before, and we shall do everything in our power to prevent the loss of them; for instance, by not risking our property, or angering our friends, or exposing our wives to temptation, or being careless about our children's health, and so on.

We often try to banish the gloom and despondency of the present by speculating upon our chances of success in the future; a process which leads us to invent a great many chimerical hopes. Every one of them contains the germ of illusion, and disappointment is inevitable when our hopes are shattered by the hard facts of life.

It is less hurtful to take the chances of misfortune as a theme for speculation; because, in doing so, we provide ourselves at once with measures of precaution against it, and a pleasant surprise when it fails to make its appearance. Is it not a fact that we always feel a marked improvement in our spirits when we begin to get over a period of anxiety? I may go further and say that there is some use in occasionally looking upon terrible misfortunes--such as might happen to us--as though they had actually happened, for then the trivial reverses which subsequently come in reality, are much easier to bear. It is a source of consolation to look back upon those great misfortunes which never happened. But in following out this rule, care must be taken not to neglect what I have said in the preceding section.

SECTION 15. The things which engage our attention--whether they are matters of business or ordinary events--are of such diverse kinds, that, if taken quite separately and in no fixed order or relation, they present a medley of the most glaring contrasts, with nothing in common, except that they one and all affect us in particular. There must be a corresponding abruptness in the thoughts and anxieties which these various matters arouse in us, if our thoughts are to be in keeping with their various subjects. Therefore, in setting about anything, the first step is to withdraw our attention from everything else: this will enable us to attend to each matter at its own time, and to enjoy or put up with it, quite apart from any thought of our remaining interests. Our thoughts must be arranged, as it were, in little drawers, so that we may open one without disturbing any of the others.

In this way we can keep the heavy burden of anxiety from weighing upon us so much as to spoil the little pleasures of the present, or from robbing us of our rest; otherwise the consideration of one matter will interfere with every other, and attention to some important business may lead us to neglect many affairs which happen to be of less moment. It is most important for everyone who is capable of higher and nobler thoughts to keep their mind from being so completely engrossed with private affairs and vulgar troubles as to let them take up all his attention and crowd out worthier matter; for that is, in a very real sense, to lose sight of the true end of life--*propter vitam vivendi perdere causas*.

Of course for this--as for so much else--self-control is necessary; without it, we cannot manage ourselves in the way I have described. And self-control may not appear so very difficult, if we consider that every man has to submit to a great deal of very severe control on the part of his surroundings, and that without it no form of existence is possible. Further, a little self-control at the right moment may prevent much subsequent compulsion at the hands of others; just as a very small section of a circle close to the centre may correspond to a part near the circumference a hundred times as large. Nothing will protect us from external compulsion so much as the control of ourselves; and, as Seneca says, to submit yourself to reason is the way to make everything else submit to you--*si tibi vis omnia subjicere, te subjice rationi*. Self-control, too, is something which we have in our own power; and if the worst comes to the worst, and it touches us in a very sensitive part, we can always relax its severity. But other people will pay no regard to our feelings, if they have to use compulsion, and we shall be treated without pity or mercy. Therefore it will be prudent to anticipate compulsion by self-control.

SECTION 16. We must set limits to our wishes, curb our desires, moderate our anger, always remembering that an individual can attain only an infinitesimal share in anything that is worth having; and that, on the other hand, everyone must incur many of the ills of life; in a word, we must bear and forbear--*abstinere et sustinere*; and if we fail to observe this rule, no position of wealth or power will prevent us from feeling wretched. This is what Horace means when he recommends us to study carefully and inquire diligently what will best promote a tranquil life--not to be always agitated by fruitless desires and fears and hopes for things, which, after all, are not worth very much:--

Inter cuncta leges et percontabere doctos Qua ratione queas traducere leniter aevum; Ne te semper inops agitet vexetque cupido, Ne pavor, et rerum mediocriter utilium spes[28].

SECTION 17. Life consists in movement, says Aristotle; and he is obviously right. We exist, physically, because our organism is the seat of constant motion; and if we are to exist intellectually, it can only be by means of continual occupation--no matter with what so long as it is some form of practical or mental activity. You may see that this is so by the way in which people who have no work or nothing to think about, immediately begin to beat the devil's tattoo with their knuckles or a stick or

---

28 Epist. I. xviii. 97.

anything that comes handy. The truth is, that our nature is essentially ***restless*** in its character: we very soon get tired of having nothing to do; it is intolerable boredom. This impulse to activity should be regulated, and some sort of method introduced into it, which of itself will enhance the satisfaction we obtain. Activity!--doing something, if possible creating something, at any rate learning something--how fortunate it is that men cannot exist without that! A man wants to use his strength, to see, if he can, what effect it will produce; and he will get the most complete satisfaction of this desire if he can make or construct something--be it a book or a basket. There is a direct pleasure in seeing work grow under one's hands day by day, until at last it is finished. This is the pleasure attaching to a work of art or a manuscript, or even mere manual labor; and, of course, the higher the work, the greater pleasure it will give.

From this point of view, those are happiest of all who are conscious of the power to produce great works animated by some significant purpose: it gives a higher kind of interest--a sort of rare flavor--to the whole of their life, which, by its absence from the life of the ordinary man, makes it, in comparison, something very insipid. For richly endowed natures, life and the world have a special interest beyond the mere everyday personal interest which so many others share; and something higher than that--a formal interest. It is from life and the world that they get the material for their works; and as soon as they are freed from the pressure of personal needs, it is to the diligent collection of material that they devote their whole existence. So with their intellect: it is to some extent of a two-fold character, and devoted partly to the ordinary affairs of every day--those matters of will which are common to them and the rest of mankind, and partly to their peculiar work--the pure and objective contemplation of existence. And while, on the stage of the world, most men play their little part and then pass away, the genius lives a double life, at once an actor and a spectator.

Let everyone, then, do something, according to the measure of his capacities. To have no regular work, no set sphere of activity--what a miserable thing it is! How often long travels undertaken for pleasure make a man downright unhappy; because the absence of anything that can be called occupation forces him, as it were, out of his right element. Effort, struggles with difficulties! that is as natural to a man as grubbing in the ground is to a mole. To have all his wants satisfied is something intolerable--the feeling of stagnation which comes from pleasures that last too long. To overcome difficulties is to experience the full delight of existence, no matter where the obstacles are encountered; whether in the affairs of life, in commerce or business; or in mental effort--the spirit of inquiry that tries to master its subject. There is always something pleasurable in the struggle and the victory. And if a man has no opportunity to excite himself, he will do what he can to create one, and according to his individual bent, he will hunt or play Cup and Ball: or led on by this unsuspected element in his nature, he will pick a quarrel with some one, or hatch a plot or intrigue, or take to swindling and rascally courses generally--all to put an end to a state of repose which is intolerable. As I have remarked, *difficilis in otio quies*--it is difficult to keep quiet if you have nothing to do.

SECTION 18. A man should avoid being led on by the phantoms of his imagination. This is not the same thing as to submit to the guidance of ideas clearly thought out: and yet these are rules of life which most people pervert. If you examine closely into the circumstances which, in any deliberation, ultimately turn the scale in favor of some particular course, you will generally find that the decision is influenced, not by any clear arrangement of ideas leading to a formal judgment, but by some fanciful picture which seems to stand for one of the alternatives in question.

In one of Voltaire's or Diderot's romances,--I forget the precise reference,--the hero, standing like a young Hercules at the parting of ways, can see no other representation of Virtue than his old tutor holding a snuff-box in his left hand, from which he takes a pinch and moralizes; whilst Vice appears in the shape of his mother's chambermaid. It is in youth, more especially, that the goal of our efforts comes to be a fanciful picture of happiness, which continues to hover before our eyes sometimes for half and even for the whole of our life--a sort of mocking spirit; for when we think our dream is to be realized, the picture fades away, leaving us the knowledge that nothing of what it promised is actually accomplished. How often this is so with the visions of domesticity--the detailed picture of what our home will be like; or, of life among our fellow-citizens or in society; or, again, of living in the country--the kind of house we shall have, its surroundings, the marks of honor and respect that will be paid to us, and so on,--whatever our hobby may be; *chaque fou a sa marotte*. It is often the same, too, with our dreams about one we love. And this is all quite natural; for the visions we conjure up affect us directly, as though they were real objects; and so they exercise a more immediate influence upon our will than an abstract idea, which gives merely a vague, general outline, devoid of details; and the details are just the real part of it. We can be only indirectly affected by an abstract idea, and yet it is the abstract idea alone which will do as much as it promises; and it is the function of education to teach us to put our trust in it. Of course the abstract idea must be occasionally explained--paraphrased, as it were--by the aid of pictures; but discreetly, *cum grano salis*.

SECTION 19. The preceding rule may be taken as a special case of the more general maxim, that a man should never let himself be mastered by the impressions of the moment, or indeed by outward appearances at all, which are incomparably more powerful in their effects than the mere play of thought or a train of ideas; not because these momentary impressions are rich in virtue of the data they supply,--it is often just the contrary,--but because they are something palpable to the senses and direct in their working; they forcibly invade our mind, disturbing our repose and shattering our resolutions.

It is easy to understand that the thing which lies before our very eyes will produce the whole of its effect at once, but that time and leisure are necessary for the working of thought and the appreciation of argument, as it is impossible to think of everything at one and the same moment. This is why we are so allured by pleasure, in spite of all our determination to resist it; or so much annoyed by a criticism, even though we know that its author it totally incompetent to judge; or so irritated by an insult, though it comes from some very contemptible quarter. In the same way, to mention no other instances, ten reasons for thinking that there is no danger may be outweighed by one mistaken notion that it is actually at hand. All this shows the radical unreason of human nature. Women frequently succumb altogether to this predominating influence of present impressions, and there are few men so overweighted with reason as to escape suffering from a similar cause.

If it is impossible to resist the effects of some external influence by the mere play of thought, the best thing to do is to neutralize it by some contrary influence; for example, the effect of an insult may be overcome by seeking the society of those who have a good opinion of us; and the unpleasant sensation of imminent danger may be avoided by fixing our attention on the means of warding it off.

Leibnitz[29] tells of an Italian who managed to bear up under the tortures of the rack by never for a moment ceasing to think of the gallows which would have awaited him, had he revealed his secret; he kept on crying out: *I see it! I see it*!--afterwards explaining that this was part of his plan.

It is from some such reason as this, that we find it so difficult to stand alone in a matter of opinion,--not to be made irresolute by the fact that everyone else disagrees with us and acts accordingly, even though we are quite sure that they are in the wrong. Take the case of a fugitive king who is trying to avoid capture; how much consolation he must find in the ceremonious and submissive attitude of a faithful follower, exhibited secretly so as not to betray his master's strict *incognito*; it must be almost necessary to prevent him doubting his own existence.

SECTION 20. In the first part of this work I have insisted upon the great value of *health* as the chief and most important element in happiness. Let me emphasize and confirm what I have there said by giving a few general rules as to its preservation.

The way to harden the body is to impose a great deal of labor and effort upon it in the days of good health,--to exercise it, both as a whole and in its several parts, and to habituate it to withstand all kinds of noxious influences. But on the appearance of an illness or disorder, either in the body as a whole or in many of its parts, a contrary course should be taken, and every means used to nurse the body, or the part of it which is affected, and to spare it any effort; for what is ailing and debilitated cannot be hardened.

The muscles may be strengthened by a vigorous use of them; but not so the nerves; they are weakened by it. Therefore, while exercising the muscles in every way that is suitable, care should be taken to spare the nerves as much as possible. The eyes, for instance, should be protected from too strong a light,--especially when it is reflected light,--from any straining of them in the dark, or from the long-continued examination of minute objects; and the ears from too loud sounds. Above all, the brain should never be forced, or used too much, or at the wrong time; let it have a rest during digestion; for then the same vital energy which forms thoughts in the brain has a great deal of work to do elsewhere,--I mean in the digestive organs, where it prepares chyme and chyle. For similar reasons, the brain should never be

---

29 *Nouveaux Essais*. Liv. I. ch. 2. Sec. 11.

used during, or immediately after, violent muscular exercise. For the motor nerves are in this respect on a par with the sensory nerves; the pain felt when a limb is wounded has its seat in the brain; and, in the same way, it is not really our legs and arms which work and move,--it is the brain, or, more strictly, that part of it which, through the medium of the spine, excites the nerves in the limbs and sets them in motion. Accordingly, when our arms and legs feel tired, the true seat of this feeling is in the brain. This is why it is only in connection with those muscles which are set in motion consciously and voluntarily,--in other words, depend for their action upon the brain,--that any feeling of fatigue can arise; this is not the case with those muscles which work involuntarily, like the heart. It is obvious, then, that injury is done to the brain if violent muscular exercise and intellectual exertion are forced upon it at the same moment, or at very short intervals.

What I say stands in no contradiction with the fact that at the beginning of a walk, or at any period of a short stroll, there often comes a feeling of enhanced intellectual vigor. The parts of the brain that come into play have had no time to become tired; and besides, slight muscular exercise conduces to activity of the respiratory organs, and causes a purer and more oxydated supply of arterial blood to mount to the brain.

It is most important to allow the brain the full measure of sleep which is required to restore it; for sleep is to a man's whole nature what winding up is to a clock[30]. This measure will vary directly with the development and activity of the brain; to overstep the measure is mere waste of time, because if that is done, sleep gains only so much in length as it loses in depth[31].

It should be clearly understood that thought is nothing but the organic function of the brain; and it has to obey the same laws in regard to exertion and repose as any other organic function. The brain can be ruined by overstrain, just like the eyes. As the function of the stomach is to digest, so it is that of the brain to think.

---

30 *Of. Welt als Wille und Vorstellung*, 4th Edition. Bk. II. pp. 236-40.

31 *Cf. loc: cit*: p. 275. Sleep is a morsel of death borrowed to keep up and renew the part of life which is exhausted by the day--*le sommeil est un emprunt fait a la mort*. Or it might be said that sleep is the interest we have to pay on the capital which is called in at death; and the higher the rate of interest and the more regularly it is paid, the further the date of redemption is postponed.

The notion of a *soul*,--as something elementary and immaterial, merely lodging in the brain and needing nothing at all for the performance of its essential function, which consists in always and unweariedly *thinking*--has undoubtedly driven many people to foolish practices, leading to a deadening of the intellectual powers; Frederick the Great, even, once tried to form the habit of doing without sleep altogether. It would be well if professors of philosophy refrained from giving currency to a notion which is attended by practical results of a pernicious character; but then this is just what professorial philosophy does, in its old-womanish endeavor to keep on good terms with the catechism. A man should accustom himself to view his intellectual capacities in no other light than that of physiological functions, and to manage them accordingly--nursing or exercising them as the case may be; remembering that every kind of physical suffering, malady or disorder, in whatever part of the body it occurs, has its effect upon the mind. The best advice that I know on this subject is given by Cabanis in his ***Rapports du physique et du moral de l'homme*[32]**.

Through neglect of this rule, many men of genius and great scholars have become weak-minded and childish, or even gone quite mad, as they grew old. To take no other instances, there can be no doubt that the celebrated English poets of the early part of this century, Scott, Wordsworth, Southey, became intellectually dull and incapable towards the end of their days, nay, soon after passing their sixtieth year; and that their imbecility can be traced to the fact that, at that period of life, they were all led on? by the promise of high pay, to treat literature as a trade and to write for money. This seduced them into an unnatural abuse of their intellectual powers; and a man who puts his Pegasus into harness, and urges on his Muse with the whip, will have to pay a penalty similar to that which is exacted by the abuse of other kinds of power.

And even in the case of Kant, I suspect that the second childhood of his last four years was due to overwork in later life, and after he had succeeded in becoming a famous man.

---

32 ***Translator's Note***. The work to which Schopenhauer here refers is a series of essays by Cabanis, a French philosopher (1757-1808), treating of mental and moral phenomena on a physiological basis. In his later days, Cabanis completely abandoned his materialistic standpoint.

Every month of the year has its own peculiar and direct influence upon health and bodily condition generally; nay, even upon the state of the mind. It is an influence dependent upon the weather.

CHAPTER III.
OUR RELATION TO OTHERS.--SECTION 21.

In making his way through life, a man will find it useful to be ready and able to do two things: to look ahead and to overlook: the one will protect him from loss and injury, the other from disputes and squabbles. No one who has to live amongst men should absolutely discard any person who has his due place in the order of nature, even though he is very wicked or contemptible or ridiculous. He must accept him as an unalterable fact--unalterable, because the necessary outcome of an eternal, fundamental principle; and in bad cases he should remember the words of Mephistopheles: es muss auch solche Kaeuze geben[33]--there must be fools and rogues in the world. If he acts otherwise, he will be committing an injustice, and giving a challenge of life and death to the man he discards. No one can alter his own peculiar individuality, his moral character, his intellectual capacity, his temperament or physique; and if we go so far as to condemn a man from every point of view, there will be nothing left him but to engage us in deadly conflict; for we are practically allowing him the right to exist only on condition that he becomes another man--which is impossible; his nature forbids it.

So if you have to live amongst men, you must allow everyone the right to exist in accordance with the character he has, whatever it turns out to be: and all you should strive to do is to make use of this character in such a way as its kind and nature permit, rather than to hope for any alteration in it, or to condemn it off-hand for what it is. This is the true sense of the maxim--Live and let live. That, however, is a task which is difficult in proportion as it is right; and he is a happy man who can once for all avoid having to do with a great many of his fellow creatures.

The art of putting up with people may be learned by practicing patience on in-

33 Goethe's *Faust*, Part I.

animate objects, which, in virtue of some mechanical or general physical necessity, oppose a stubborn resistance to our freedom of action--a form of patience which is required every day. The patience thus gained may be applied to our dealings with men, by accustoming ourselves to regard their opposition, wherever we encounter it, as the inevitable outcome of their nature, which sets itself up against us in virtue of the same rigid law of necessity as governs the resistance of inanimate objects. To become indignant at their conduct is as foolish as to be angry with a stone because it rolls into your path. And with many people the wisest thing you can do, is to re-solve to make use of those whom you cannot alter.

SECTION 22. It is astonishing how easily and how quickly similarity, or dif-ference of mind and disposition, makes itself felt between one man and another as soon as they begin to talk: every little trifle shows it. When two people of totally different natures are conversing, almost everything said by the one will, in a greater or less degree, displease the other, and in many cases produce positive annoyance; even though the conversation turn upon the most out-of-the-way subject, or one in which neither of the parties has any real interest. People of similar nature, on the other hand, immediately come to feel a kind of general agreement; and if they are cast very much in the same mould, complete harmony or even unison will flow from their intercourse.

This explain two circumstances. First of all, it shows why it is that common, ordinary people are so sociable and find good company wherever they go. Ah! those good, dear, brave people. It is just the contrary with those who are not of the com-mon run; and the less they are so, the more unsociable they become; so that if, in their isolation, they chance to come across some one in whose nature they can find even a single sympathetic chord, be it never so minute, they show extraordinary pleasure in his society. For one man can be to another only so much as the other is to him. Great minds are like eagles, and build their nest in some lofty solitude.

Secondly, we are enabled to understand how it is that people of like disposi-tion so quickly get on with one another, as though they were drawn together by magnetic force--kindred souls greeting each other from afar. Of course the most frequent opportunity of observing this is afforded by people of vulgar tastes and inferior intellect, but only because their name is legion; while those who are better off in this respect and of a rarer nature, are not often to be met with: they are called rare because you can seldom find them.

Take the case of a large number of people who have formed themselves into a league for the purpose of carrying out some practical object; if there be two rascals among them, they will recognize each other as readily as if they bore a similar badge, and will at once conspire for some misfeasance or treachery. In the same way, if you can imagine--*per impossible*--a large company of very intelligent and clever people, amongst whom there are only two blockheads, these two will be sure to be drawn together by a feeling of sympathy, and each of them will very soon secretly rejoice at having found at least one intelligent person in the whole company. It is really quite curious to see how two such men, especially if they are morally and intellectually of an inferior type, will recognize each other at first sight; with what zeal they will strive to become intimate; how affably and cheerily they will run to greet each other, just as though they were old friends;--it is all so striking that one is tempted to embrace the Buddhist doctrine of metempsychosis and presume that they were on familiar terms in some former state of existence.

Still, in spite of all this general agreement, men are kept apart who might come together; or, in some cases, a passing discord springs up between them. This is due to diversity of mood. You will hardly ever see two people exactly in the same frame of mind; for that is something which varies with their condition of life, occupation, surroundings, health, the train of thought they are in at the moment, and so on. These differences give rise to discord between persons of the most harmonious disposition. To correct the balance properly, so as to remove the disturbance--to introduce, as it were, a uniform temperature,--is a work demanding a very high degree of culture. The extent to which uniformity of mood is productive of good-fellowship may be measured by its effects upon a large company. When, for instance, a great many people are gathered together and presented with some objective interest which works upon all alike and influences them in a similar way, no matter what it be--a common danger or hope, some great news, a spectacle, a play, a piece of music, or anything of that kind--you will find them roused to a mutual expression of thought, and a display of sincere interest. There will be a general feeling of pleasure amongst them; for that which attracts their attention produces a unity of mood by overpowering all private and personal interests.

And in default of some objective interest of the kind I have mentioned, recourse is usually had to something subjective. A bottle of wine is not an uncommon means of introducing a mutual feeling of fellowship; and even tea and coffee are used for a like end.

The discord which so easily finds its way into all society as an effect of the different moods in which people happen to be for the moment, also in part explains why it is that memory always idealizes, and sometimes almost transfigures, the attitude we have taken up at any period of the past--a change due to our inability to remember all the fleeting influences which disturbed us on any given occasion. Memory is in this respect like the lens of a *camera obscura*: it contracts everything within its range, and so produces a much finer picture than the actual landscape affords. And, in the case of a man, absence always goes some way towards securing this advantageous light; for though the idealizing tendency of the memory requires times to complete its work, it begins it at once. Hence it is a prudent thing to see your friends and acquaintances only at considerable intervals of time; and on meeting them again, you will observe that memory has been at work.

SECTION 23. No man can see *over his own height.* Let me explain what I mean.

You cannot see in another man any more than you have in yourself; and your own intelligence strictly determines the extent to which he comes within its grasp. If your intelligence is of a very low order, mental qualities in another, even though they be of the highest kind, will have no effect at all upon you; you will see nothing in their possessor except the meanest side of his individuality--in other words, just those parts of his character and disposition which are weak and defective. Your whole estimate of the man will be confined to his defects, and his higher mental qualities will no more exist for you than colors exist for those who cannot see.

Intellect is invisible to the man who has none. In any attempt to criticise another's work, the range of knowledge possessed by the critic is as essential a part of his verdict as the claims of the work itself.

Hence intercourse with others involves a process of leveling down. The qualities which are present in one man, and absent in another, cannot come into play when they meet; and the self-sacrifice which this entails upon one of the parties, calls forth no recognition from the other.

Consider how sordid, how stupid, in a word, how *vulgar* most men are, and you will see that it is impossible to talk to them without becoming vulgar yourself for the time being. Vulgarity is in this respect like electricity; it is easily distributed. You will then fully appreciate the truth and propriety of the expression, **to make yourself cheap**; and you will be glad to avoid the society of people whose only possible point of contact with you is just that part of your nature of which you have least reason to be proud. So you will see that, in dealing with fools and blockheads, there is only one way of showing your intelligence--by having nothing to do with them. That means, of course, that when you go into society, you may now and then feel like a good dancer who gets an invitation to a ball, and on arriving, finds that everyone is lame:--with whom is he to dance?

SECTION 24. I feel respect for the man--and he is one in a hundred--who, when he is waiting or sitting unoccupied, refrains from rattling or beating time with anything that happens to be handy,--his stick, or knife and fork, or whatever else it may be. The probability is that he is thinking of something.

With a large number of people, it is quite evident that their power of sight completely dominates over their power of thought; they seem to be conscious of existence only when they are making a noise; unless indeed they happen to be smoking, for this serves a similar end. It is for the same reason that they never fail to be all eyes and ears for what is going on around them.

SECTION 25. La Rochefoucauld makes the striking remark that it is difficult to feel deep veneration and great affection for one and the same person. If this is so, we shall have to choose whether it is veneration or love that we want from our fellow-men.

Their love is always selfish, though in very different ways; and the means used to gain it are not always of a kind to make us proud. A man is loved by others mainly in the degree in which he moderates his claim on their good feeling and intelligence: but he must act genuinely in the matter and without dissimulation--not merely out of forbearance, which is at bottom a kind of contempt. This calls to mind a very true observation of Helvetius[34]: **the amount of intellect necessary to please**

34　**Translator's Note**. Helvetius, Claude-Adrien (1715-71), a French philosophical writer much esteemed by Schopenhauer. His chief work, **De l'Esprit**, excited great interest and opposition at the time of its publication, on account of the author's pronounced materialism.

us, is a most accurate measure of the amount of intellect we have ourselves. With these remarks as premises, it is easy to draw the conclusion.

Now with veneration the case is just the opposite; it is wrung from men reluctantly, and for that very reason mostly concealed. Hence, as compared with love, veneration gives more real satisfaction; for it is connected with personal value, and the same is not directly true of love, which is subjective in its nature, whilst veneration is objective. To be sure, it is more useful to be loved than to be venerated.

SECTION 26. Most men are so thoroughly subjective that nothing really interests them but themselves. They always think of their own case as soon as ever any remark is made, and their whole attention is engrossed and absorbed by the merest chance reference to anything which affects them personally, be it never so remote: with the result that they have no power left for forming an objective view of things, should the conversation take that turn; neither can they admit any validity in arguments which tell against their interest or their vanity. Hence their attention is easily distracted. They are so readily offended, insulted or annoyed, that in discussing any impersonal matter with them, no care is too great to avoid letting your remarks bear the slightest possible reference to the very worthy and sensitive individuals whom you have before you; for anything you may say will perhaps hurt their feelings. People really care about nothing that does not affect them personally. True and striking observations, fine, subtle and witty things are lost upon them: they cannot understand or feel them. But anything that disturbs their petty vanity in the most remote and indirect way, or reflects prejudicially upon their exceedingly precious selves--to that, they are most tenderly sensitive. In this respect they are like the little dog whose toes you are so apt to tread upon inadvertently--you know it by the shrill bark it sets up: or, again, they resemble a sick man covered with sores and boils, with whom the greatest care must be taken to avoid unnecessary handling. And in some people this feeling reaches such a pass that, if they are talking with anyone, and he exhibits, or does not sufficiently conceal, his intelligence and discernment, they look upon it as a downright insult; although for the moment they hide their ill will, and the unsuspecting author of it afterwards ruminates in vain upon their conduct, and racks his brain to discover what he could possibly have done to excite their malice and hatred.

But it is just as easy to flatter and win them over; and this is why their judgment is usually corrupt, and why their opinions are swayed, not by what is really true and right, but by the favor of the party or class to which they belong. And the ultimate reason of it all is, that in such people force of will greatly predominates over knowledge; and hence their meagre intellect is wholly given up to the service of the will, and can never free itself from that service for a moment.

Astrology furnishes a magnificent proof of this miserable subjective tendency in men, which leads them to see everything only as bearing upon themselves, and to think of nothing that is not straightway made into a personal matter. The aim of astrology is to bring the motions of the celestial bodies into relation with the wretched *Ego* and to establish a connection between a comet in the sky and squabbles and rascalities on earth[35].

SECTION 27. When any wrong statement is made, whether in public or in society, or in books, and well received--or, at any rate, not refuted--that that is no reason why you should despair or think there the matter will rest. You should comfort yourself with the reflection that the question will be afterwards gradually subjected to examination; light will be thrown upon it; it will be thought over, considered, discussed, and generally in the end the correct view will be reached; so that, after a time--the length of which will depend upon the difficulty of the subject--everyone will come to understand that which a clear head saw at once.

In the meantime, of course, you must have patience. He who can see truly in the midst of general infatuation is like a man whose watch keeps good time, when all clocks in the town in which he lives are wrong. He alone knows the right time; but what use is that to him? for everyone goes by the clocks which speak false, not even excepting those who know that his watch is the only one that is right.

SECTION 28. Men are like children, in that, if you spoil them, they become naughty.

Therefore it is well not to be too indulgent or charitable with anyone. You may take it as a general rule that you will not lose a friend by refusing him a loan, but that you are very likely to do so by granting it; and, for similar reasons, you will not readily alienate people by being somewhat proud and careless in your behaviour; but if you are very kind and complaisant towards them, you will often make them arrogant and intolerable, and so a breach will ensue.

---

35   See, for instance, Stobasus, *Eclog. I*. xxii. 9.

There is one thing that, more than any other, throws people absolutely off their balance--the thought that you are dependent upon them. This is sure to produce an insolent and domineering manner towards you. There are some people, indeed, who become rude if you enter into any kind of relation with them; for instance, if you have occasion to converse with them frequently upon confidential matters, they soon come to fancy that they can take liberties with you, and so they try and transgress the laws of politeness. This is why there are so few with whom you care to become more intimate, and why you should avoid familiarity with vulgar people. If a man comes to think that I am more dependent upon him than he is upon me, he at once feels as though I had stolen something from him; and his endeavor will be to have his vengeance and get it back. The only way to attain superiority in dealing with men, is to let it be seen that you are independent of them.

And in this view it is advisable to let everyone of your acquaintance--whether man or woman--feel now and then that you could very well dispense with their company. This will consolidate friendship. Nay, with most people there will be no harm in occasionally mixing a grain of disdain with your treatment of them; that will make them value your friendship all the more. *Chi non istima vien stimato*, as a subtle Italian proverb has it--to disregard is to win regard. But if we really think very highly of a person, we should conceal it from him like a crime. This is not a very gratifying thing to do, but it is right. Why, a dog will not bear being treated too kindly, let alone a man!

SECTION 29. It is often the case that people of noble character and great mental gifts betray a strange lack of worldly wisdom and a deficiency in the knowledge of men, more especially when they are young; with the result that it is easy to deceive or mislead them; and that, on the other hand, natures of the commoner sort are more ready and successful in making their way in the world.

The reason of this is that, when a man has little or no experience, he must judge by his own antecedent notions; and in matters demanding judgment, an antecedent notion is never on the same level as experience. For, with the commoner sort of people, an antecedent notion means just their own selfish point of view. This is not the case with those whose mind and character are above the ordinary; for it is precisely in this respect--their unselfishness--that they differ from the rest of mankind; and as they judge other people's thoughts and actions by their own high standard, the result does not always tally with their calculation.

But if, in the end, a man of noble character comes to see, as the effect of his own experience, or by the lessons he learns from others, what it is that may be expected of men in general,--namely, that five-sixths of them are morally and intellectually so constituted that, if circumstances do not place you in relation with them, you had better get out of their way and keep as far as possible from having anything to do with them,--still, he will scarcely ever attain an adequate notion of their wretchedly mean and shabby nature: all his life long he will have to be extending and adding to the inferior estimate he forms of them; and in the meantime he will commit a great many mistakes and do himself harm.

Then, again, after he has really taken to heart the lessons that have been taught him, it will occasionally happen that, when he is in the society of people whom he does not know, he will be surprised to find how thoroughly reasonable they all appear to be, both in their conversation and in their demeanor--in fact, quite honest, sincere, virtuous and trustworthy people, and at the same time shrewd and clever.

But that ought not to perplex him. Nature is not like those bad poets, who, in setting a fool or a knave before us, do their work so clumsily, and with such evident design, that you might almost fancy you saw the poet standing behind each of his characters, and continually disavowing their sentiments, and telling you in a tone of warning: *This is a knave; that is a fool; do not mind what he says*. But Nature goes to work like Shakespeare and Goethe, poets who make every one of their characters--even if it is the devil himself!--appear to be quite in the right for the moment that they come before us in their several parts; the characters are described so objectively that they excite our interest and compel us to sympathize with their point of view; for, like the works of Nature, every one of these characters is evolved as the result of some hidden law or principle, which makes all they say and do appear natural and therefore necessary. And you will always be the prey or the plaything of the devils and fools in this world, if you expect to see them going about with horns or jangling their bells.

And it should be borne in mind that, in their intercourse with others, people are like the moon, or like hunchbacks; they show you only one of their sides. Every man has an innate talent for mimicry,--for making a mask out of his physiognomy, so that he can always look as if he really were what he pretends to be; and since he makes his calculations always within the lines of his individual nature, the appearance he puts on suits him to a nicety, and its effect is extremely deceptive. He dons his mask whenever his object is to flatter himself into some one's good opinion; and you may pay just as much attention to it as if it were made of wax or cardboard, never forgetting that excellent Italian proverb: ***non e si tristo cane che non meni la coda***,--there is no dog so bad but that he will wag his tail.

In any case it is well to take care not to form a highly favorable opinion of a person whose acquaintance you have only recently made, for otherwise you are very likely to be disappointed; and then you will be ashamed of yourself and perhaps even suffer some injury. And while I am on the subject, there is another fact that deserves mention. It is this. A man shows his character just in the way in which he deals with trifles,--for then he is off his guard. This will often afford a good opportunity of observing the boundless egoism of man's nature, and his total lack of consideration for others; and if these defects show themselves in small things, or merely in his general demeanor, you will find that they also underlie his action in matters of importance, although he may disguise the fact. This is an opportunity which should not be missed. If in the little affairs of every day,--the trifles of life, those matters to which the rule ***de minimis non*** applies,--a man is inconsiderate and seeks only what is advantageous or convenient to himself, to the prejudice of others' rights; if he appropriates to himself that which belongs to all alike, you may be sure there is no justice in his heart, and that he would be a scoundrel on a wholesale scale, only that law and compulsion bind his hands. Do not trust him beyond your door. He who is not afraid to break the laws of his own private circle, will break those of the State when he can do so with impunity.

If the average man were so constituted that the good in him outweighed the bad, it would be more advisable to rely upon his sense of justice, fairness, gratitude, fidelity, love or compassion, than to work upon his fears; but as the contrary is the case, and it is the bad that outweighs the good, the opposite course is the more prudent one.

If any person with whom we are associated or have to do, exhibits unpleasant or annoying qualities, we have only to ask ourselves whether or not this person is of so much value to us that we can put up with frequent and repeated exhibitions of the same qualities in a somewhat aggravated form[36]. In case of an affirmative answer to this question, there will not be much to be said, because talking is very little use. We must let the matter pass, with or without some notice; but we should neverthe-less remember that we are thereby exposing ourselves to a repetition of the offence. If the answer is in the negative, we must break with our worthy friend at once and forever; or in the case of a servant, dismiss him. For he will inevitably repeat the offence, or do something tantamount to it, should the occasion return, even though for the moment he is deep and sincere in his assurances of the contrary. There is nothing, absolutely nothing, that a man cannot forget,--but not **himself, his own character**. For character is incorrigible; because all a man's actions emanate from an inward principle, in virtue of which he must always do the same thing under like circumstances; and he cannot do otherwise. Let me refer to my prize essay on the so-called **Freedom of the Will**, the perusal of which will dissipate any delusions the reader may have on this subject.

To become reconciled to a friend with whom you have broken, is a form of weakness; and you pay the penalty of it when he takes the first opportunity of doing precisely the very thing which brought about the breach; nay, he does it the more boldly, because he is secretly conscious that you cannot get on without him. This is also applicable to servants whom you have dismissed, and then taken into your service again.

For the same reason, you should just as little expect people to continue to act in a similar way under altered circumstances. The truth is that men alter their de-meanor and sentiments just as fast as their interest changes; and their resign in this respect is a bill drawn for short payment that the man must be still more short-sighted who accepts the bill without protesting it. Accordingly, suppose you want to know how a man will behave in an office into which you think of putting him; you should not build upon expectations, on his promises or assurances. For, even allowing that he is quite sincere, he is speaking about a matter of which he has no knowledge. The only way to calculate how he will behave, is to consider the cir-cumstances in which he will be placed, and the extent to which they will conflict with his character.

If you wish to get a clear and profound insight--and it is very needful--into

---

36   To **forgive and forget** means to throw away dearly bought experience.

the true but melancholy elements of which most men are made, you will find in a very instructive thing to take the way they behave in the pages of literature as a commentary to their doings in practical life, and *vice versa.* The experience thus gained will be very useful in avoiding wrong ideas, whether about yourself or about others. But if you come across any special trait of meanness or stupidity--in life or in literature,--you must be careful not to let it annoy or distress you, but to look upon it merely as an addition to your knowledge--a new fact to be considered in studying the character of humanity. Your attitude towards it will be that of the mineralogist who stumbles upon a very characteristic specimen of a mineral.

Of course there are some facts which are very exceptional, and it is difficult to understand how they arise, and how it is that there come to be such enormous differences between man and man; but, in general, what was said long ago is quite true, and the world is in a very bad way. In savage countries they eat one another, in civilized they deceive one another; and that is what people call the way of the world! What are States and all the elaborate systems of political machinery, and the rule of force, whether in home or in foreign affairs,--what are they but barriers against the boundless iniquity of mankind? Does not all history show that whenever a king is firmly planted on a throne, and his people reach some degree of prosperity, he uses it to lead his army, like a band of robbers, against adjoining countries? Are not almost all wars ultimately undertaken for purposes of plunder? In the most remote antiquity, and to some extent also in the Middle Ages, the conquered became slaves,--in other words, they had to work for those who conquered them; and where is the difference between that and paying war-taxes, which represent the product of our previous work?

All war, says Voltaire, is a matter of robbery; and the Germans should take that as a warning.

SECTION 30. No man is so formed that he can be left entirely to himself, to go his own ways; everyone needs to be guided by a preconceived plan, and to follow certain general rules. But if this is carried too far, and a man tries to take on a character which is not natural or innate in him, but it artificially acquired and evolved merely by a process of reasoning, he will very soon discover that Nature cannot be forced, and that if you drive it out, it will return despite your efforts:--

Naturam expelles furca, tamen usque recurret.

To understand a rule governing conduct towards others, even to discover it for oneself and to express it neatly, is easy enough; and still, very soon afterwards, the rule may be broken in practice. But that is no reason for despair; and you need not fancy that as it is impossible to regulate your life in accordance with abstract ideas and maxims, it is better to live just as you please. Here, as in all theoretical instruction that aims at a practical result, the first thing to do is to understand the rule; the second thing is to learn the practice of it. The theory may be understand at once by an effort of reason, and yet the practice of it acquired only in course of time.

A pupil may lean the various notes on an instrument of music, or the different position in fencing; and when he makes a mistake, as he is sure to do, however hard he tries, he is apt to think it will be impossible to observe the rules, when he is set to read music at sight or challenged to a furious duel. But for all that, gradual practice makes him perfect, through a long series of slips, blunders and fresh efforts. It is just the same in other things; in learning to write and speak Latin, a man will forget the grammatical rules; it is only by long practice that a blockhead turns into a courtier, that a passionate man becomes shrewd and worldly-wise, or a frank person reserved, or a noble person ironical. But though self-discipline of this kind is the result of long habit, it always works by a sort of external compulsion, which Nature never ceases to resist and sometimes unexpectedly overcomes. The difference between action in accordance with abstract principles, and action as the result of original, innate tendency, is the same as that between a work of art, say a watch--where form and movement are impressed upon shapeless and inert matter--and a living organism, where form and matter are one, and each is inseparable from the other.

There is a maxim attributed to the Emperor Napoleon, which expresses this relation between acquired and innate character, and confirms what I have said: ***everything that is unnatural is imperfect***;--a rule of universal application, whether in the physical or in the moral sphere. The only exception I can think of to this rule is aventurine[37], a substance known to mineralogists, which in its natural state can-

---

37 ***Translator's Note***. Aventurine is a rare kind of quartz; and the same name is given to a brownish-colored glass much resembling it, which is manufactured at Murano. It is so called from the fact that the glass was discovered by chance (arventura).

not compare with the artificial preparation of it.

And in this connection let me utter a word of protest against any and every form of **affectation**. It always arouses contempt; in the first place, because it argues deception, and the deception is cowardly, for it is based on fear; and, secondly, it argues self-condemnation, because it means that a man is trying to appear what he is not, and therefore something which he things better than he actually is. To affect a quality, and to plume yourself upon it, is just to confess that you have not got it. Whether it is courage, or learning, or intellect, or wit, or success with women, or riches, or social position, or whatever else it may be that a man boasts of, you may conclude by his boasting about it that that is precisely the direction in which he is rather weak; for if a man really possesses any faculty to the full, it will not occur to him to make a great show of affecting it; he is quite content to know that he has it. That is the application of the Spanish proverb: **herradura que chacolotea clavo le falta**--a clattering hoof means a nail gone. To be sure, as I said at first, no man ought to let the reins go quite loose, and show himself just as he is; for there are many evil and bestial sides to our nature which require to be hidden away out of sight; and this justifies the negative attitude of dissimulation, but it does not justify a positive feigning of qualities which are not there. It should also be remembered that affectation is recognized at once, even before it is clear what it is that is being affected. And, finally, affectation cannot last very long, and one day the mask will fall off. **Nemo potest personam diu ferre fictam**, says Seneca[38]; **ficta cito in naturam suam recidunt**--no one can persevere long in a fictitious character; for nature will soon reassert itself.

SECTION 31. A man bears the weight of his own body without knowing it, but he soon feels the weight of any other, if he tries to move it; in the same way, a man can see other people's shortcoming's and vices, but he is blind to his own. This arrangement has one advantage: it turns other people into a kind of mirror, in which a man can see clearly everything that is vicious, faulty, ill-bred and loathsome in his own nature; only, it is generally the old story of the dog barking at is own image; it is himself that he sees and not another dog, as he fancies.

He who criticises others, works at the reformation of himself. Those who form the secret habit of scrutinizing other people's general behavior, and passing severe

---

38 *De Clementia, I.* 1.

judgment upon what they do and leave undone, thereby improve themselves, and work out their own perfection: for they will have sufficient sense of justice, or at any rate enough pride and vanity, to avoid in their own case that which they condemn so harshly elsewhere. But tolerant people are just the opposite, and claim for themselves the same indulgence that they extend to others--*hanc veniam damus petimusque vicissim*. It is all very well for the Bible to talk about the mote in another's eye and the beam in one's own. The nature of the eye is to look not at itself but at other things; and therefore to observe and blame faults in another is a very suitable way of becoming conscious of one's own. We require a looking-glass for the due dressing of our morals.

The same rule applies in the case of style and fine writing. If, instead of condemning, you applaud some new folly in these matters, you will imitate it. That is just why literary follies have such vogue in Germany. The Germans are a very tolerant people--everybody can see that! Their maxim is--*Hanc veniam damns petimusque vicissim.*

SECTION 32. When he is young, a man of noble character fancies that the relations prevailing amongst mankind, and the alliances to which these relations lead, are at bottom and essentially, *ideal* in their nature; that is to say, that they rest upon similarity of disposition or sentiment, or taste, or intellectual power, and so on.

But, later on, he finds out that it is a *real* foundation which underlies these alliances; that they are based upon some *material* interest. This is the true foundation of almost all alliances: nay, most men have no notion of an alliance resting upon any other basis. Accordingly we find that a man is always measured by the office he holds, or by his occupation, nationality, or family relations--in a word, by the position and character which have been assigned him in the conventional arrangements of life, where he is ticketed and treated as so much goods. Reference to what he is in himself, as a man--to the measure of his own personal qualities--is never made unless for convenience' sake: and so that view of a man is something exceptional, to be set aside and ignored, the moment that anyone finds it disagreeable; and this is what usually happens. But the more of personal worth a man has, the less pleasure he will take in these conventional arrangements; and he will try to withdraw from the sphere in which they apply. The reason why these arrangements exist at all, is simply that in this world of ours misery and need are the chief features: therefore it is everywhere the essential and paramount business of life to devise the means of alleviating them.

SECTION 33. As paper-money circulates in the world instead of real coin, so, is the place of true esteem and genuine friendship, you have the outward appearance of it--a mimic show made to look as much like the real thing as possible.

On the other hand, it may be asked whether there are any people who really deserve the true coin. For my own part, I should certainly pay more respect to an honest dog wagging his tail than to a hundred such demonstrations of human regard.

True and genuine friendship presupposes a strong sympathy with the weal and woe of another--purely objective in its character and quite disinterested; and this in its turn means an absolute identification of self with the object of friendship. The egoism of human nature is so strongly antagonistic to any such sympathy, that true friendship belongs to that class of things--the sea-serpent, for instance,--with regard to which no one knows whether they are fabulous or really exist somewhere or other.

Still, in many cases, there is a grain of true and genuine friendship in the relation of man to man, though generally, of course, some secret personal interest is at the bottom of them--some one among the many forms that selfishness can take. But in a world where all is imperfect, this grain of true feeling is such an ennobling influence that it gives some warrant for calling those relations by the name of friendship, for they stand far above the ordinary friendships that prevail amongst mankind. The latter are so constituted that, were you to hear how your dear friends speak of you behind your back, you would never say another word to them.

Apart from the case where it would be a real help to you if your friend were to make some great sacrifice to serve you, there is no better means of testing the genuineness of his feelings than the way in which he receives the news of a misfortune that has just happened to you. At that moment the expression of his features will either show that his one thought is that of true and sincere sympathy for you; or else the absolute composure of his countenance, or the passing trace of something other than sympathy, will confirm the well-known maxim of La Rochefoucauld: *Dans l'adversite de nos meilleurs amis, nous trouvons toujours quelque chose qui ne nous deplait pas*. Indeed, at such a moment, the ordinary so-called friend will find it hard to suppress the signs of a slight smile of pleasure. There are few ways by which you can make more certain of putting people into a good humor than by telling them of some trouble that has recently befallen you, or by unreservedly disclosing some personal weakness of yours. How characteristic this is of humanity!

Distance and long absence are always prejudicial to friendship, however disinclined a man may be to admit. Our regard for people whom we do not see--even though they be our dearest friends--gradually dries up in the course of years, and they become abstract notions; so that our interest in them grows to be more and more intellectual,--nay, it is kept up only as a kind of tradition; whilst we retain a lively and deep interest in those who are constantly before our eyes, even if they be only pet animals. This shows how much men are limited by their senses, and how true is the remark that Goethe makes in *Tasso* about the dominant influence of the present moment:--

> *Die Gegenwart ist eine maechtige Goettin*[39]

Friends of the house are very rightly so called; because they are friends of the house rather than of its master; in other words, they are more like cats than dogs.

Your friends will tell you that they are sincere; your enemies are really so. Let your enemies' censure be like a bitter medicine, to be used as a means of self-knowledge.

A friend in need, as the saying goes, is rare. Nay, it is just the contrary; no sooner have you made a friend than he is in need, and asks for a loan.

SECTION 34. A man must be still a greenhorn in the ways of the world, if he imagines that he can make himself popular in society by exhibiting intelligence and discernment. With the immense majority of people, such qualities excite hatred and resentment, which are rendered all the harder to bear by the fact that people are obliged to suppress--even from themselves--the real reason of their anger.

What actually takes place is this. A man feels and perceives that the person with whom he is conversing is intellectually very much his superior[40].

---

39   Act iv., se. 4.

40   Cf. *Welt als Wills und Vorstellung*, Bk. II. p. 256 (4th Edit.), where I quote from Dr. Johnson, and from Merck, the friend of Goethe's youth. The former says: *There is nothing by which a man exasperates most people more, than by displaying a*

He thereupon secretly and half unconsciously concludes that his interlocutor must form a proportionately low and limited estimate of his abilities. That is a method of reasoning--an enthymeme--which rouses the bitterest feelings of sullen and rancorous hatred. And so Gracian is quite right in saying that the only way to win affection from people is to show the most animal-like simplicity of demeanor--*para ser bien quisto, el unico medio vestirse la piel del mas simple de los brutos*[41].

To show your intelligence and discernment is only an indirect way of reproaching other people for being dull and incapable. And besides, it is natural for a vulgar man to be violently agitated by the sight of opposition in any form; and in this case envy comes in as the secret cause of his hostility. For it is a matter of daily observation that people take the greatest pleasure in that which satisfies their vanity; and vanity cannot be satisfied without comparison with others. Now, there is nothing of which a man is prouder than of intellectual ability, for it is this that gives him his commanding place in the animal world. It is an exceedingly rash thing to let any one see that you are decidedly superior to him in this respect, and to let other people see it too; because he will then thirst for vengeance, and generally look about for an opportunity of taking it by means of insult, because this is to pass from the sphere of *intellect* to that of *will*--and there, all are on an equal footing as regards the feeling of hostility. Hence, while rank and riches may always reckon upon deferential treatment in society, that is something which intellectual ability can never expect; to be ignored is the greatest favor shown to it; and if people notice it at all, it is because they regard it as a piece of impertinence, or else as something to which *superior ability of brilliancy in conversation. They seem pleased at the time, but their envy makes them curse him at their hearts.* (Boswells *Life of Johnson* aetat: 74).

41 *Translator's Note*.--Balthazar Graeian, *Oraculo manual, y arte de prudencia*, 240. Gracian (1584-1658) was a Spanish prose writer and Jesuit, whose works deal chiefly with the observation of character in the various phenomena of life. Schopenhauer, among others, had a great admiration for his worldly philosophy, and translated his *Oraculo manual*--a system of rules for the conduct of life--into German. The same book was translated into English towards the close of the seventeenth century.

its possessor has no legitimate right, and upon which he dares to pride himself; and in retaliation and revenge for his conduct, people secretly try and humiliate him in some other way; and if they wait to do this, it is only for a fitting opportunity. A man may be as humble as possible in his demeanor, and yet hardly ever get people to overlook his crime in standing intellectually above them. In the **Garden of Roses**, Sadi makes the remark:-- **You should know that foolish people are a hundredfold more averse to meeting the wise than the wise are indisposed for the company of the foolish**.

On the other hand, it is a real recommendation to be stupid. For just as warmth is agreeable to the body, so it does the mind good to feel its superiority; and a man will seek company likely to give him this feeling, as instinctively as he will approach the fireplace or walk in the sun if he wants to get warm. But this means that he will be disliked on account of his superiority; and if a man is to be liked, he must really be inferior in point of intellect; and the same thing holds good of a woman in point of beauty. To give proof of real and unfeigned inferiority to some of the people you meet--that is a very difficult business indeed!

Consider how kindly and heartily a girl who is passably pretty will welcome one who is downright ugly. Physical advantages are not thought so much of in the case of man, though I suppose you would rather a little man sat next to you than one who was bigger than yourself. This is why, amongst men, it is the dull and ignorant, and amongst women, the ugly, who are always popular and in request[42].

---

42   If you desire to get on in the world, friends and acquaintances are by far the best passport to fortune. The possession of a great deal of ability makes a man proud, and therefore not apt to flatter those who have very little, and from whom, on that account, the possession of great ability should be carefully concealed. The consciousness of small intellectual power has just the opposite effect, and is very compatible with a humble, affable and companionable nature, and with respect for what is mean and wretched. This is why an inferior sort of man has so many friends to befriend and encourage him.

These remarks are applicable not only to advancement in political life, but to all competition for places of honor and dignity, nay, even for reputation in the world of science, literature and art. In learned societies, for example, mediocrity--that very acceptable quality--is always to the fore, whilst merit meets with tardy recog-

It is likely to be said of such people that they are extremely good-natured, because every one wants to find a pretext for caring about them--a pretext which will blind both himself and other people to the real reason why he likes them. This is also why mental superiority of any sort always tends to isolate its possessor; people run away from him out of pure hatred, and say all manner of bad things about him by way of justifying their action. Beauty, in the case of women, has a similar effect: very pretty girls have no friends of their own sex, and they even find it hard to get another girl to keep them company. A handsome woman should always avoid applying for a position as companion, because the moment she enters the room, her prospective mistress will scowl at her beauty, as a piece of folly with which, both for her own and for her daughter's sake, she can very well dispense. But if the girl has advantages of rank, the case is very different; because rank, unlike personal qualities which work by the force of mere contrast, produces its effect by a process of reflection; much in the same way as the particular hue of a person's complexion depends upon the prevailing tone of his immediate surroundings.

SECTION 35. Our trust in other people often consists in great measure of pure laziness, selfishness and vanity on our own part: I say *laziness*, because, instead of making inquiries ourselves, and exercising an active care, we prefer to trust others; *selfishness*, because we are led to confide in people by the pressure of our own affairs; and *vanity*, when we ask confidence for a matter on which we rather pride ourselves. And yet, for all that, we expect people to be true to the trust we repose in them.

But we ought not to become angry if people put no trust in us: because that really means that they pay honesty the sincere compliment of regarding it as a very rare thing,--so rare, indeed, as to leave us in doubt whether its existence is not merely fabulous.

SECTION 36. *Politeness*,--which the Chinese hold to be a cardinal virtue,--is based upon two considerations of policy. I have explained one of these considerations in my *Ethics*; the other is as follows:--Politeness is a tacit agreement that people's miserable defects, whether moral or intellectual, shall on either side be ignored and not made the subject of reproach; and since these defects are thus ren-

---

nition, or with none at all. So it is in everything.

dered somewhat less obtrusive, the result is mutually advantageous[43].

It is a wise thing to be polite; consequently, it is a stupid thing to be rude. To make enemies by unnecessary and willful incivility, is just as insane a proceeding as to set your house on fire. For politeness is like a counter--an avowedly false coin, with which it is foolish to be stingy. A sensible man will be generous in the use of it. It is customary in every country to end a letter with the words:--*your most obedient servant--votre tres-humble serviteur--suo devotissimo servo*. (The Germans are the only people who suppress the word *servant--Diener--*because, of course, it is not true!) However, to carry politeness to such an extent as to damage your prospects, is like giving money where only counters are expected.

Wax, a substance naturally hard and brittle, can be made soft by the application of a little warmth, so that it will take any shape you please. In the same way, by being polite and friendly, you can make people pliable and obliging, even though they are apt to be crabbed and malevolent. Hence politeness is to human nature what warmth is to wax.

Of course, it is no easy matter to be polite; in so far, I mean, as it requires us to show great respect for everybody, whereas most people deserve none at all; and again in so far as it demands that we should feign the most lively interest in people, when we must be very glad that we have nothing to do with them. To combine politeness with pride is a masterpiece of wisdom.

We should be much less ready to lose our temper over an insult,--which, in the strict sense of the word, means that we have not been treated with respect,--if, on the one hand, we have not such an exaggerated estimate of our value and dignity--that is to say, if we were not so immensely proud of ourselves; and, on the other hand, if we had arrived at any clear notion of the judgment which, in his heart, one man generally passes upon another. If most people resent the slightest

---

43 *Translator's Note.*--In the passage referred to (Grundlage der Moral, collected works, Vol. IV., pp. 187 and 198), Schopenhauer explains politeness as a conventional and systematic attempt to mask the egoism of human nature in the small affairs of life,--an egoism so repulsive that some such device is necessary for the purpose of concealing its ugliness. The relation which politeness bears to the true love of one's neighbor is analogous to that existing between justice as an affair of legality, and justice as the real integrity of the heart.

hint that any blame attaches to them, you may imagine their feelings if they were to overhear what their acquaintance say about them. You should never lose sight of the fact that ordinary politeness is only a grinning mask: if it shifts its place a little, or is removed for a moment, there is no use raising a hue and cry. When a man is downright rude, it is as though he had taken off all his clothes, and stood before you in *puris naturalibus*. Like most men in this condition, he does not present a very attractive appearance.

SECTION 37. You ought never to take any man as a model for what you should do or leave undone; because position and circumstances are in no two cases alike, and difference of character gives a peculiar, individual tone to what a man does. Hence *duo cum faciunt idem, non est idem*--two persons may do the same thing with a different result. A man should act in accordance with his own character, as soon as he has carefully deliberated on what he is about to do.

The outcome of this is that *originality* cannot be dispensed with in practical matters: otherwise, what a man does will not accord with what he is.

SECTION 38. Never combat any man's opinion; for though you reached the age of Methuselah, you would never have done setting him right upon all the absurd things that he believes.

It is also well to avoid correcting people's mistakes in conversation, however good your intentions may be; for it is easy to offend people, and difficult, if not impossible, to mend them.

If you feel irritated by the absurd remarks of two people whose conversation you happen to overhear, you should imagine that you are listening to a dialogue of two fools in a comedy. *Probatum est.*

The man who comes into the world with the notion that he is really going to instruct in matters of the highest importance, may thank his stars if he escapes with a whole skin.

SECTION 39. If you want your judgment to be accepted, express it coolly and without passion. All violence has its seat in the *will*; and so, if your judgment is expressed with vehemence, people will consider it an effort of will, and not the outcome of knowledge, which is in its nature cold and unimpassioned. Since the will is the primary and radical element in human nature, and *intellect* merely supervenes as something secondary, people are more likely to believe that the opinion you express with so much vehemence is due to the excited state of your will, rather than that the excitement of the will comes only from the ardent nature of your opinion.

SECTION 40. Even when you are fully justified in praising yourself, you should never be seduced into doing so. For vanity is so very common, and merit so very uncommon, that even if a man appears to be praising himself, though very indirectly, people will be ready to lay a hundred to one that he is talking out of pure vanity, and that he has not sense enough to see what a fool he is making of himself.

Still, for all that, there may be some truth in Bacon's remark that, as in the case of calumny, if you throw enough dirt, some of it will stick, so it it also in regard to self-praise; with the conclusion that self-praise, in small doses, is to be recommended[44].

SECTION 41. If you have reason to suspect that a person is telling you a lie, look as though you believed every word he said. This will give him courage to go on; he will become more vehement in his assertions, and in the end betray himself.

Again, if you perceive that a person is trying to conceal something from you, but with only partial success, look as though you did not believe him, This opposition on your part will provoke him into leading out his reserve of truth and bringing the whole force of it to bear upon your incredulity.

SECTION 42. You should regard all your private affairs as secrets, and, in respect of them, treat your acquaintances, even though you are on good terms with them, as perfect strangers, letting them know nothing more than they can see for themselves. For in course of time, and under altered circumstances, you may find it a disadvantage that they know even the most harmless things about you.

And, as a general rule, it is more advisable to show your intelligence by saying nothing than by speaking out; for silence is a matter of prudence, whilst speech has something in it of vanity. The opportunities for displaying the one or the other

---

44 *Translator's Note*.--Schopenhauer alludes to the following passage in Bacon's **De Augmentis Scientiarum**, Bk. viii., ch. 2: **Sicut enim dici solet de calumnia**, audacter calumniare, semper aliquid haeret; sic dici potest de jactantia, (nisi plane deformis fuerit et ridicula), audacter te vendita, semper aliquid haeret. **Haerebit certe apud populum, licet prudentiores subrideant. Itaque existimatio parta apud plurimos paucorum fastidium abunde compensabit.**

quality occur equally often; but the fleeting satisfaction afforded by speech is often preferred to the permanent advantage secured by silence.

The feeling of relief which lively people experience in speaking aloud when no one is listening, should not be indulged, lest it grow into a habit; for in this way thought establishes such very friendly terms with speech, that conversation is apt to become a process of thinking aloud. Prudence exacts that a wide gulf should be fixed between what we think and what we say.

At times we fancy that people are utterly unable to believe in the truth of some statement affecting us personally, whereas it never occurs to them to doubt it; but if we give them the slightest opportunity of doubting it, they find it absolutely impossible to believe it any more. We often betray ourselves into revealing something, simply because we suppose that people cannot help noticing it,--just as a man will throw himself down from a great height because he loses his head, in other words, because he fancies that he cannot retain a firm footing any longer; the torment of his position is so great, that he thinks it better to put an end to it at once. This is the kind of insanity which is called *acrophobia*.

But it should not be forgotten how clever people are in regard to affairs which do not concern them, even though they show no particularly sign of acuteness in other matters. This is a kind of algebra in which people are very proficient: give them a single fact to go upon, and they will solve the most complicated problems. So, if you wish to relate some event that happened long ago, without mentioning any names, or otherwise indicating the persons to whom you refer, you should be very careful not to introduce into your narrative anything that might point, however distantly, to some definite fact, whether it is a particular locality, or a date, or the name of some one who was only to a small extent implicated, or anything else that was even remotely connected with the event; for that at once gives people something positive to go upon, and by the aid of their talent for this sort of algebra, they will discover all the rest. Their curiosity in these matters becomes a kind of enthusiasm: their will spurs on their intellect, and drives it forward to the attainment of the most remote results. For however unsusceptible and different people may be to general and universal truths, they are very ardent in the matter of particular details.

In keeping with what I have said, it will be found that all those who profess to give instructions in the wisdom of life are specially urgent in commending the practice of silence, and assign manifold reasons why it should be observed; so it is not necessary for me to enlarge upon the subject any further. However, I may just add one or two little known Arabian proverbs, which occur to me as peculiarly appropriate:--

Do not tell a friend anything that you would conceal from an enemy.

A secret is in my custody, if I keep it; but should it escape me, it is I who am the prisoner.

The tree of silence bears the fruit of peace.

SECTION 43. Money is never spent to so much advantage as when you have been cheated out of it; for at one stroke you have purchased prudence.

SECTION 44. If possible, no animosity should be felt for anyone. But carefully observe and remember the manner in which a man conducts himself, so that you may take the measure of his value,--at any rate in regard to yourself,--and regulate your bearing towards him accordingly; never losing sight of the fact that character is unalterable, and that to forget the bad features in a man's disposition is like throwing away hard-won money. Thus you will protect yourself against the results of unwise intimacy and foolish friendship.

Give way neither to love nor to hate, is one-half of worldly wisdom: *say nothing and believe nothing*, the other half. Truly, a world where there is need of such rules as this and the following, is one upon which a man may well turn his back.

SECTION 45. To speak angrily to a person, to show your hatred by what you say or by the way you look, is an unnecessary proceeding--dangerous, foolish, ridiculous, and vulgar.

Anger and hatred should never be shown otherwise than in what you do; and feelings will be all the more effective in action, in so far as you avoid the exhibition of them in any other way. It is only cold-blooded animals whose bite is poisonous.

SECTION 46. To speak without emphasizing your words--*parler sans accent*--is an old rule with those who are wise in the world's ways. It means that you should leave other people to discover what it is that you have said; and as their minds are slow, you can make your escape in time. On the other hand, to emphasize your meaning--*parler avec accent*--is to address their feelings; and the result is always the opposite of what you expect. If you are polite enough in your manner and courteous in your tone there are many people whom you may abuse outright, and yet run no immediate risk of offending them.

CHAPTER IV,
WORLDLY FORTUNE.--SECTION 47.

However varied the forms that human destiny may take, the same elements are always present; and so life is everywhere much of a piece, whether it passed in the cottage or in the palace, in the barrack or in the cloister. Alter the circumstance as much as you please! point to strange adventures, successes, failures! life is like a sweet-shop, where there is a great variety of things, odd in shape and diverse in color--one and all made from the same paste. And when men speak of some one's success, the lot of the man who has failed is not so very different as it seems. The inequalities in the world are like the combinations in a kaleidoscope; at every turn a fresh picture strikes the eye; and yet, in reality, you see only the same bits of glass as you saw before.

SECTION 48. An ancient writer says, very truly, that there are three great powers in the world; *Sagacity, Strength*, and *Luck*,--[Greek: sunetos, kratos, tuchu.] I think the last is the most efficacious.

A man's life is like the voyage of a ship, where luck--*secunda aut adversa fortuna*--acts the part of the wind, and speeds the vessel on its way or drives it far out of its course. All that the man can do for himself is of little avail; like the rudder, which, if worked hard and continuously, may help in the navigation of the ship; and yet all may be lost again by a sudden squall. But if the wind is only in the right quarter, the ship will sail on so as not to need any steering. The power of luck is nowhere better expressed than in a certain Spanish proverb: *Da Ventura a tu hijo, y echa lo en el mar*--give your son luck and throw him into the sea.

Still, chance, it may be said, is a malignant power, and as little as possible should be left to its agency. And yet where is there any giver who, in dispensing gifts, tells us quite clearly that we have no right to them, and that we owe them not to any merit on our part, but wholly to the goodness and grace of the giver--at the same time allowing us to cherish the joyful hope of receiving, in all humility, further undeserved gifts from the same hands--where is there any giver like that, unless it be *Chance*? who understands the kingly art of showing the recipient that all merit is powerless and unavailing against the royal grace and favor.

On looking back over the course of his life,--that *labyrinthine way of error*,--a man must see many points where luck failed him and misfortune came; and then it is easy to carry self-reproach to an unjust excess. For the course of a man's life is in no wise entirely of his own making; it is the product of two factors--the series of things that happened, and his own resolves in regard to them, and these two are constantly interacting upon and modifying each other. And besides these, another influence is at work in the very limited extent of a man's horizon, whether it is that he cannot see very far ahead in respect of the plans he will adopt, or that he is still less able to predict the course of future events: his knowledge is strictly confined to present plans and present events. Hence, as long as a man's goal is far off, he cannot steer straight for it; he must be content to make a course that is approximately right; and in following the direction in which he thinks he ought to go, he will often have occasion to tack.

All that a man can do is to form such resolves as from time to time accord with the circumstances in which he is placed, in the hope of thus managing to advance a step nearer towards the final goal. It is usually the case that the position in which we stand, and the object at which we aim, resemble two tendencies working with dissimilar strength in different directions; and the course of our life is represented by their diagonal, or resultant force.

Terence makes the remark that life is like a game at dice, where if the number that turns up is not precisely the one you want, you can still contrive to use it equally:--*in vita est hominum quasi cum ludas tesseris; si illud quod maxime opus est jactu non cadit, illud quod cecidit forte, id arte ut corrigas*[45]. Or, to put the matter more shortly, life is a game of cards, when the cards are shuffled and dealt by fate. But for my present purpose, the most suitable simile would be that of a game of chess, where the plan we determined to follow is conditioned by the play

---

45 He seems to have been referring to a game something like backgammon

of our rival,--in life, by the caprice of fate. We are compelled to modify our tactics, often to such an extent that, as we carry them out, hardly a single feature of the original plan can be recognized.

But above and beyond all this, there is another influence that makes itself felt in our lives. It is a trite saying--only too frequently true--that we are often more foolish than we think. On the other hand, we are often wiser than we fancy our-selves to be. This, however, is a discovery which only those can make, of whom it is really true; and it takes them a long time to make it. Our brains are not the wis-est part of us. In the great moments of life, when a man decides upon an important step, his action is directed not so much by any clear knowledge of the right thing to do, as by an inner impulse--you may almost call it an instinct--proceeding from the deepest foundations of his being. If, later on, he attempts to criticise his action by the light of hard and fast ideas of what is right in the abstract--those unprofit-able ideas which are learnt by rote, or, it may be, borrowed from other people; if he begins to apply general rules, the principles which have guided others, to his own case, without sufficiently weighing the maxim that one man's meat is another's poison, then he will run great risk of doing himself an injustice. The result will show where the right course lay. It is only when a man has reached the happy age of wisdom that he is capable of just judgment in regard either to his own actions or to those of others.

It may be that this impulse or instinct is the unconscious effect of a kind of prophetic dream which is forgotten when we awake--lending our life a uniformity of tone, a dramatic unity, such as could never result from the unstable moments of consciousness, when we are so easily led into error, so liable to strike a false note. It is in virtue of some such prophetic dream that a man feels himself called to great achievements in a special sphere, and works in that direction from his youth up out of an inner and secret feeling that that is his true path, just as by a similar instinct the bee is led to build up its cells in the comb. This is the impulse which Balthazar Gracian calls *la gran sinderesis*[46]--the great power of moral discernment:

---

46 *Translator's Note*.--This obscure word appears to be derived from the Greek *sug-taereo* (N.T. and Polyb.) meaning "to observe strictly." It occurs in *The Doctor and Student*, a series of dialogues between a doctor of divinity and a student on the laws of England, first published in 1518; and is there (Dialog. I. ch. 13) explained as "a

it is something that a man instinctively feels to be his salvation without which he were lost.

To act in accordance with abstract principles is a difficult matter, and a great deal of practice will be required before you can be even occasionally successful; it of tens happens that the principles do not fit in with your particular case. But every man has certain innate *concrete principles*--a part, as it were, of the very blood that flows in his veins, the sum or result, in fact, of all his thoughts, feelings and volitions. Usually he has no knowledge of them in any abstract form; it is only when he looks back upon the course his life has taken, that he becomes aware of having been always led on by them--as though they formed an invisible clue which he had followed unawares.

SECTION 49. That Time works great changes, and that all things are in their nature fleeting--these are truths that should never be forgotten. Hence, in whatever case you may be, it is well to picture to yourself the opposite: in prosperity, to be mindful of misfortune; in friendship, of enmity; in good weather, of days when the sky is overcast; in love, of hatred; in moments of trust, to imagine the betrayal that will make you regret your confidence; and so, too, when you are in evil plight, to have a lively sense of happier times--what a lasting source of true worldly wisdom were there! We should then always reflect, and not be so very easily deceived; because, in general, we should anticipate the very changes that the years will bring.

Perhaps in no form of knowledge is personal experience so indispensable as in learning to see that all things are unstable and transitory in this world. There is nothing that, in its own place and for the time it lasts, is not a product of necessity, and therefore capable of being fully justified; and it is this fact that makes circum-

---

natural power of the soule, set in the highest part thereof, moving and stirring it to good, and abhoring evil." This passage is copied into Milton's Commonplace Book, edit. *Horwood*, Sec. 79. The word is also found in the Dictionary of the Spanish Academy (vol. vi. of the year 1739) in the sense of an innate discernment of moral principles, where a quotation is given from Madre Maria de Jesus, abbess of the convent of the Conception at Agreda, a mystical writer of the seventeenth century, frequently consulted by Philip IV.,--and again in the Bolognese Dictionary of 1824, with a similar meaning, illustrated from the writings of Salvini (1653-1729). For these references I am indebted to the kindness of Mr. Norman Maccoll.

stances of every year, every month, even of every day, seem as though they might maintain their right to last to all eternity. But we know that this can never be the case, and that in a world where all is fleeting, change alone endures. He is a prudent man who is not only undeceived by apparent stability, but is able to forecast the lines upon which movement will take place[47].

But people generally think that present circumstances will last, and that matters will go on in the future as they have clone in the past. Their mistakes arises from the fact that they do not understand the cause of the things they see--causes which, unlike the effects they produce, contain in themselves the germ of future change. The effects are all that people know, and they hold fast to them on the supposition that those unknown causes, which were sufficient to bring them about, will also be able to maintain them as they are. This is a very common error; and the fact that it is common is not without its advantage, for it means that people always err in unison; and hence the calamity which results from the error affects all alike, and is therefore easy to bear; whereas, if a philosopher makes a mistake, he is alone in his error, and so at a double disadvantage[48].

But in saying that we should anticipate the effects of time, I mean that we should mentally forecast what they are likely to be; I do not mean that we should practically forestall them, by demanding the immediate performance of promises which time alone can fulfill. The man who makes his demand will find out that there is no worse or more exacting usurer than Time; and that, if you compel Time

---

47 *Chance* plays so great a part in all human affairs that when a man tries to ward off a remote danger by present sacrifice, the danger often vanishes under some new and unforeseen development of events; and then the sacrifice, in addition to being a complete loss, brings about such an altered state of things as to be in itself a source of positive danger in the face of this new development. In taking measures of precaution, then, it is well not to look too far ahead, but to reckon with chance; and often to oppose a courageous front to a danger, in the hope that, like many a dark thunder-cloud, it may pass away without breaking.

48 I may remark, parenthetically, that all this is a confirmation of the principle laid down in *Die Welt als Wille und Vorstellung* (Bk. I. p. 94: 4th edit.), that error always consists in making *a wrong inference*, that is, in ascribing a given effect to something that did not cause it.

to give money in advance, you will have to pay a rate of interest more ruinous than any Jew would require. It is possible, for instance, to make a tree burst forth into leaf, blossom, or even bear fruit within a few days, by the application of unslaked lime and artificial heat; but after that the tree will wither away. So a young man may abuse his strength--it may be only for a few weeks--by trying to do at nineteen what he could easily manage at thirty, and Time may give him the loan for which he asks; but the interest he will have to pay comes out of the strength of his later years; nay, it is part of his very life itself.

There are some kinds of illness in which entire restoration to health is possible only by letting the complaint run its natural course; after which it disappears without leaving any trace of its existence. But if the sufferer is very impatient, and, while he is still affected, insists that he is completely well, in this case, too, Time will grant the loan, and the complaint may be shaken off; but life-long weakness and chronic mischief will be the interest paid upon it.

Again, in time of war or general disturbance, a man may require ready money at once, and have to sell out his investments in land or consols for a third or even a still smaller fraction of the sum he would have received from them, if he could have waited for the market to right itself, which would have happened in due course; but he compels Time to grant him a loan, and his loss is the interest he has to pay. Or perhaps he wants to go on a long journey and requires the money: in one or two years he could lay by a sufficient sum out of his income, but he cannot afford to wait; and so he either borrows it or deducts it from his capital; in other words, he gets Time to lend him the money in advance. The interest he pays is a disordered state of his accounts, and permanent and increasing deficits, which he can never make good.

Such is Time's usury; and all who cannot wait are its victims. There is no more thriftless proceeding than to try and mend the measured pace of Time. Be careful, then, not to become its debtor.

SECTION 50. In the daily affairs of life, you will have very many opportunities of recognizing a characteristic difference between ordinary people of prudence and discretion. In estimating the possibility of danger in connection with any undertaking, an ordinary man will confine his inquiries to the kind of risk that has already attended such undertakings in the past; whereas a prudent person will look ahead, and consider everything that might possibly happen in the future, having regard to a certain Spanish maxim: *lo que no acaece en un ano, acaece en un rato*--a thing may not happen in a year, and yet may happen within two minutes.

The difference in question is, of course, quite natural; for it requires some amount of discernment to calculate possibilities; but a man need only have his senses about him to see what has already happened.

Do not omit to sacrifice to evil spirits. What I mean is, that a man should not hesitate about spending time, trouble, and money, or giving up his comfort, or restricting his aims and denying himself, if he can thereby shut the door on the possibility of misfortune. The most terrible misfortunes are also the most improbable and remote--the least likely to occur. The rule I am giving is best exemplified in the practice of insurance,--a public sacrifice made on the altar of anxiety. Therefore take out your policy of insurance!

SECTION 51. Whatever fate befalls you, do not give way to great rejoicings or great lamentations; partly because all things are full of change, and your fortune may turn at any moment; partly because men are so apt to be deceived in their judgment as to what is good or bad for them.

Almost every one in his turn has lamented over something which afterwards turned out to be the very best thing for him that could have happened--or rejoiced at an event which became the source of his greatest sufferings. The right state of mind has been finely portrayed by Shakespeare:

I have felt so many quirks of joy and grief That the first face of neither, on the start, Can woman me unto't[49].

And, in general, it may be said that, if a man takes misfortunes quietly, it is because he knows that very many dreadful things may happen in the course of life; and so he looks upon the trouble of the moment as only a very small part of that which might come. This is the Stoic temper--never to be unmindful of the sad fate of humanity--*condicionis humanoe oblitus*; but always to remember that our existence is full of woe and misery: and that the ills to which we are exposed are innumerable. Wherever he be, a man need only cast a look around, to revive the sense of human misery: there before his eyes he can see mankind struggling and floundering in torment,--all for the sake of a wretched existence, barren and unprofitable!

---

49 *All's Well that Ends Well, Act. ii. Sc. 2*.

If he remembers this, a man will not expect very much from life, but learn to accommodate himself to a world where all is relative and no perfect state exists;--always looking misfortune in the face, and if he cannot avoid it, meeting it with courage.

It should never be forgotten that misfortune, be it great or small, is the element in which we live. But that is no reason why a man should indulge in fretful complaints, and, like Beresford[50], pull a long face over the *Miseries of Human Life*,--and not a single hour is free from them; or still less, call upon the Deity at every flea-bite--*in pulicis morsu Deum invocare*. Our aim should be to look well about us, to ward off misfortune by going to meet it, to attain such perfection and refinement in averting the disagreeable things of life,--whether they come from our fellow-men or from the physical world,--that, like a clever fox, we may slip out of the way of every mishap, great or small; remembering that a mishap is generally only our own awkwardness in disguise.

The main reason why misfortune falls less heavily upon us, if we have looked upon its occurrence as not impossible, and, as the saying is, prepared ourselves for it, may be this: if, before this misfortune comes, we have quietly thought over it as something which may or may not happen, the whole of its extent and range is known to us, and we can, at least, determine how far it will affect us; so that, if it really arrives, it does not depress us unduly--its weight is not felt to be greater than it actually is. But if no preparation has been made to meet it, and it comes unexpectedly, the mind is in a state of terror for the moment and unable to measure the full extent of the calamity; it seems so far-reaching in its effects that the victim might well think there was no limit to them; in any case, its range is exaggerated. In the same way, darkness and uncertainty always increase the sense of danger. And, of course, if we have thought over the possibility of misfortune, we have also at the same time considered the sources to which we shall look for help and consolation; or, at any rate, we have accustomed ourselves to the idea of it.

There is nothing that better fits us to endure the misfortunes of life with com-

---

50 *Translator's Note*.--Rev. James Beresford (1764-1840), miscellaneous writer. The full title of this, his chief work, is "The Miseries of Human Life; or the last groans of Timothy Testy and Samuel Sensitive, with a few supplementary sighs from Mrs. Testy."

posure, than to know for certain that *everything that happens--from the smallest up to the greatest facts of existence--happens of necessity*[51]. A man soon accommodates himself to the inevitable--to something that must be; and if he knows that nothing can happen except of necessity, he will see that things cannot be other that they are, and that even the strangest chances in the world are just as much a product of necessity as phenomena which obey well-known rules and turn out exactly in accordance with expectation. Let me here refer to what I have said elsewhere on the soothing effect of the knowledge that all things are inevitable and a product of necessity[52].

If a man is steeped in the knowledge of this truth, he will, first of all, do what he can, and then readily endure what he must.

We may regard the petty vexations of life that are constantly happening, as designed to keep us in practice for bearing great misfortunes, so that we may not become completely enervated by a career of prosperity. A man should be as Siegfried, armed *cap-a-pie*, towards the small troubles of every day--those little differences we have with our fellow-men, insignificant disputes, unbecoming conduct in other people, petty gossip, and many other similar annoyances of life; he should not feel them at all, much less take them to heart and brood over them, but hold them at arm's length and push them out of his way, like stones that lie in the road, and upon no account think about them and give them a place in his reflections.

SECTION 52. What people commonly call *Fate* is, as a general rule, nothing but their own stupid and foolish conduct. There is a fine passage in Homer[53], illustrating the truth of this remark, where the poet praises [GREEK: maetis]--shrewd council; and his advice is worthy of all attention. For if wickedness is atoned for only in another world, stupidity gets its reward here--although, now and then, mercy may be shown to the offender.

It is not ferocity but cunning that strikes fear into the heart and forebodes danger; so true it is that the human brain is a more terrible weapon than the lion's

51   This is a truth which I have firmly established in my prize-essay on the *Freedom of the Will*, where the reader will find a detailed explanation of the grounds on which it rests. Cf. especially p. 60. [Schopenhauer's Works, 4th Edit., vol. iv.-- *Tr.*]

52   Cf. *Welt als Wille und Vorstellung*, Bk. I. p. 361 (4th edit.).

53   *Iliad*, xxiii. 313, sqq.

paw.

The most finished man of the world would be one who was never irresolute and never in a hurry.

SECTION 53. *Courage* comes next to prudence as a quality of mind very essential to happiness. It is quite true that no one can endow himself with either, since a man inherits prudence from his mother and courage from his father; still, if he has these qualities, he can do much to develop them by means of resolute exercise.

In this world, *where the game is played with loaded dice*, a man must have a temper of iron, with armor proof to the blows of fate, and weapons to make his way against men. Life is one long battle; we have to fight at every step; and Voltaire very rightly says that if we succeed, it is at the point of the sword, and that we die with the weapon in our hand--on *ne reussit dans ce monde qua la pointe de l'epee, et on meurt les armes a la main*. It is a cowardly soul that shrinks or grows faint and despondent as soon as the storm begins to gather, or even when the first cloud appears on the horizon. Our motto should be *No Surrender*; and far from yielding to the ills of life, let us take fresh courage from misfortune:--

Tu ne cede malis sed contra audentior ito[54].

As long as the issue of any matter fraught with peril is still in doubt, and there is yet some possibility left that all may come right, no one should ever tremble or think of anything but resistance,--just as a man should not despair of the weather if he can see a bit of blue sky anywhere. Let our attitude be such that we should not quake even if the world fell in ruins about us:--

Si fractus illabatur orbis   Impavidum ferient ruinae[55].

Our whole life itself--let alone its blessings--would not be worth such a cowardly trembling and shrinking of the heart. Therefore, let us face life courageously and show a firm front to every ill:--

---

54 Virgil, *Aeneid*, vi. 95.
55 Horace, Odes iii. 3.

Quocirca vivite fortes Fortiaque adversis opponite pectora rebus.

Still, it is possible for courage to be carried to an excess and to degenerate into rashness. It may even be said that some amount of fear is necessary, if we are to exist at all in the world, and cowardice is only the exaggerated form of it. This truth has been very well expressed by Bacon, in his account of **Terror Panicus**; and the etymological account which he gives of its meaning, is very superior to the ancient explanation preserved for us by Plutarch[56]. He connects the expression with **Pan** the personification of Nature[57]; and observes that fear is innate in every living thing, and, in fact, tends to its preservation, but that it is apt to come into play without due cause, and that man is especially exposed to it. The chief feature of this **Panie Terror** is that there is no clear notion of any definite danger bound up with it; that it presumes rather than knows that danger exists; and that, in case of need, it pleads fright itself as the reason for being afraid.

---

56 *De Iside et Osiride* ch. 14.

57 *De Sapientia Veterum*, C. 6. Natura enim rerum omnibus viventibus indidit mentum ac formidinem, vitae atque essentiae suae conservatricem, ac mala ingruentia vitantem et depellentem. Verumtamen eaden natura modum tenere nescia est: sed timoribus salutaribus semper vanos et innanes admiscet; adeo ut omnia (si intus conspici darentur) Panicis terroribus plenissima sint praesertim humana.

CHAPTER V.
THE AGES OF LIFE.

There is a very fine saying of Voltaire's to the effect that every age of life has its own peculiar mental character, and that a man will feel completely unhappy if his mind is not in accordance with his years:--

Qui n'a pas l'esprit de son age,
De son age atout le malheur.

It will, therefore, be a fitting close to our speculations upon the nature of happiness, if we glance at the chances which the various periods of life produce in us.

Our whole life long it is *the present*, and the present alone, that we actually possess: the only difference is that at the beginning of life we look forward to a long future, and that towards the end we look back upon a long past; also that our temperament, but not our character, undergoes certain well-known changes, which make *the present* wear a different color at each period of life.

I have elsewhere stated that in childhood we are more given to using our *intellect* than our *will*; and I have explained why this is so[58]. It is just for this reason that the first quarter of life is so happy: as we look back upon it in after years, it seems a sort of lost paradise. In childhood our relations with others are limited, our wants

---

58 *Translator's Note*.--Schopenhauer refers to *Die Welt als Wille und Vorstellung*, Bk. II. c, 31, p. 451 (4th edit.), where he explains that this is due to the fact that at that period of life the brain and nervous system are much more developed than any other part of the organism.

are few,--in a word, there is little stimulus for the will; and so our chief concern is the extension of our knowledge. The intellect--like the brain, which attains its full size in the seventh year[59], is developed early, though it takes time to mature; and it explores the whole world of its surroundings in its constant search for nutriment: it is then that existence is in itself an ever fresh delight, and all things sparkle with the charm of novelty.

This is why the years of childhood are like a long poem. For the function of poetry, as of all art, is to grasp the *Idea*--in the Platonic sense; in other words, to apprehend a particular object in such a way as to perceive its essential nature, the characteristics it has in common with all other objects of the same kind; so that a single object appears as the representative of a class, and the results of one experience hold good for a thousand.

It may be thought that my remarks are opposed to fact, and that the child is never occupied with anything beyond the individual objects or events which are presented to it from time to time, and then only in so far as they interest and excite its will for the moment; but this is not really the case. In those early years, life--in the full meaning of the word, is something so new and fresh, and its sensations are so keen and unblunted by repetition, that, in the midst of all its pursuits and without any clear consciousness of what it is doing, the child is always silently occupied in grasping the nature of life itself,--in arriving at its fundamental character and general outline by means of separate scenes and experiences; or, to use Spinoza's phraseology, the child is learning to see the things and persons about it *sub specie aeternitatis*,--as particular manifestations of universal law.

The younger we are, then, the more does every individual object represent for us the whole class to which it belongs; but as the years increase, this becomes less and less the case. That is the reason why youthful impressions are so different from those of old age. And that it also why the slight knowledge and experience gained in childhood and youth afterwards come to stand as the permanent rubric, or head-

---

59   *Translator's Note*.--This statement is not quite correct. The weight of the brain increases rapidly up to the seventh year, more slowly between the sixteenth and the twentieth year, still more slowly till between thirty and forty years of age, when it attains its maximum. At each decennial period after this, it is supposed to decrease in weight on the average, an ounce for every ten years.

ing, for all the knowledge acquired in later life,--those early forms of knowledge passing into categories, as it were, under which the results of subsequent experience are classified; though a clear consciousness of what is being done, does not always attend upon the process.

In this way the earliest years of a man's life lay the foundation of his view of the world, whether it be shallow or deep; and although this view may be extended and perfected later on, it is not materially altered. It is an effect of this purely objective and therefore poetical view of the world,--essential to the period of childhood and promoted by the as yet undeveloped state of the volitional energy--that, as children, we are concerned much more with the acquisition of pure knowledge than with exercising the power of will. Hence that grave, fixed look observable in so many children, of which Raphael makes such a happy use in his depiction of cherubs, especially in the picture of the *Sistine Madonna*. The years of childhood are thus rendered so full of bliss that the memory of them is always coupled with longing and regret.

While we thus eagerly apply ourselves to learning the outward aspect of things, as the primitive method of understanding the objects about us, education aims at instilling into us *ideas*. But ideas furnish no information as to the real and essential nature of objects, which, as the foundation and true content of all knowledge, can be reached only by the process called *intuition*. This is a kind of knowledge which can in no wise be instilled into us from without; we must arrive at it by and for ourselves.

Hence a man's intellectual as well as his moral qualities proceed from the depths of his own nature, and are not the result of external influences; and no educational scheme--of Pestalozzi, or of any one else--can turn a born simpleton into a man of sense. The thing is impossible! He was born a simpleton, and a simpleton he will die.

It is the depth and intensity of this early intuitive knowledge of the external world that explain why the experiences of childhood take such a firm hold on the memory. When we were young, we were completely absorbed in our immediate surroundings; there was nothing to distract our attention from them; we looked upon the objects about us as though they were the only ones of their kind, as though, indeed, nothing else existed at all. Later on, when we come to find out how many things there are in the world, this primitive state of mind vanishes, and with it our patience.

I have said elsewhere[60] that the world, considered as ***object***,--in other words, as it is ***presented*** to us objectively,--wears in general a pleasing aspect; but that in the world, considered as ***subject***,--that is, in regard to its inner nature, which is ***will***,--pain and trouble predominate. I may be allowed to express the matter, briefly, thus: ***the world is glorious to look at, but dreadful in reality***.

Accordingly, we find that, in the years of childhood, the world is much better known to us on its outer or objective side, namely, as the presentation of will, than on the side of its inner nature, namely, as the will itself. Since the objective side wears a pleasing aspect, and the inner or subjective side, with its tale of horror, remains as yet unknown, the youth, as his intelligence develops, takes all the forms of beauty that he sees, in nature and in art, for so many objects of blissful existence; they are so beautiful to the outward eye that, on their inner side, they must, he thinks, be much more beautiful still. So the world lies before him like another Eden; and this is the Arcadia in which we are all born.

A little later, this state of mind gives birth to a thirst for real life--the impulse to do and suffer--which drives a man forth into the hurly-burly of the world. There he learns the other side of existence--the inner side, the will, which is thwarted at every step. Then comes the great period of disillusion, a period of very gradual growth; but once it has fairly begun, a man will tell you that he has got over all his false notions--*l'age des illusions est passe*; and yet the process is only beginning, and it goes on extending its sway and applying more and more to the whole of life.

So it may be said that in childhood, life looks like the scenery in a theatre, as you view it from a distance; and that in old age it is like the same scenery when you come up quite close to it.

And, lastly, there is another circumstance that contributes to the happiness of childhood. As spring commences, the young leaves on the trees are similar in color and much the same in shape; and in the first years of life we all resemble one another and harmonize very well. But with puberty divergence begins; and, like the radii of a circle, we go further and further apart.

60 ***Die Welt als Wille und Vorstellung***, Bk. II. c. 31, p. 426-7 (4th Edit.), to which the reader is referred for a detailed explanation of my meaning.

The period of youth, which forms the remainder of this earlier half of our existence--and how many advantages it has over the later half!--is troubled and made miserable by the pursuit of happiness, as though there were no doubt that it can be met with somewhere in life,--a hope that always ends in failure and leads to discontent. An illusory image of some vague future bliss--born of a dream and shaped by fancy--floats before our eyes; and we search for the reality in vain. So it is that the young man is generally dissatisfied with the position in which he finds himself, whatever it may be; he ascribes his disappointment solely to the state of things that meets him on his first introduction to life, when he had expected something very different; whereas it is only the vanity and wretchedness of human life everywhere that he is now for the first time experiencing.

It would be a great advantage to a young man if his early training could eradicate the idea that the world has a great deal to offer him. But the usual result of education is to strengthen this delusion; and our first ideas of life are generally taken from fiction rather than from fact.

In the bright dawn of our youthful days, the poetry of life spreads out a gorgeous vision before us, and we torture ourselves by longing to see it realized. We might as well wish to grasp the rainbow! The youth expects his career to be like an interesting romance; and there lies the germ of that disappointment which I have been describing[61]. What lends a charm to all these visions is just the fact that they are visionary and not real, and that in contemplating them we are in the sphere of pure knowledge, which is sufficient in itself and free from the noise and struggle of life. To try and realize those visions is to make them an object of ***will***--a process which always involves pain[62].

If the chief feature of the earlier half of life is a never-satisfied longing after happiness, the later half is characterized by the dread of misfortune. For, as we advance in years, it becomes in a greater or less degree clear that all happiness is chimerical in its nature, and that pain alone is real. Accordingly, in later years, we, or, at least, the more prudent amongst us, are more intent upon eliminating what is painful from our lives and making our position secure, than on the pursuit of

---

61 Cf. loc. cit., p. 428.

62 Let me refer the reader, if he is interested in the subject, to the volume already cited, chapter 37.

positive pleasure. I may observe, by the way, that in old age, we are better able to prevent misfortunes from coming, and in youth better able to bear them when they come.

In my young days, I was always pleased to hear a ring at my door: ah! thought I, now for something pleasant. But in later life my feelings on such occasions were rather akin to dismay than to pleasure: heaven help me! thought I, what am I to do? A similar revulsion of feeling in regard to the world of men takes place in all persons of any talent or distinction. For that very reason they cannot be said properly to belong to the world; in a greater or less degree, according to the extent of their superiority, they stand alone. In their youth they have a sense of being abandoned by the world; but later on, they feel as though they had escaped it. The earlier feeling is an unpleasant one, and rests upon ignorance; the second is pleasurable--for in the meantime they have come to know what the world is.

The consequence of this is that, as compared with the earlier, the later half of life, like the second part of a musical period, has less of passionate longing and more restfulness about it. And why is this the case Simply because, in youth, a man fancies that there is a prodigious amount of happiness and pleasure to be had in the world, only that it is difficult to come by it; whereas, when he becomes old, he knows that there is nothing of the kind; he makes his mind completely at ease on the matter, enjoys the present hour as well as he can, and even takes a pleasure in trifles.

The chief result gained by experience of life is *clearness of view*. This is what distinguishes the man of mature age, and makes the world wear such a different aspect from that which it presented in his youth or boyhood. It is only then that he sees things quite plain, and takes them for that which they really are: while in earlier years he saw a phantom-world, put together out of the whims and crotchets of his own mind, inherited prejudice and strange delusion: the real world was hidden from him, or the vision of it distorted. The first thing that experience finds to do is to free us from the phantoms of the brain--those false notions that have been put into us in youth.

To prevent their entrance at all would, of course, be the best form of education, even though it were only negative in aim: but it would be a task full of difficulty. At first the child's horizon would have to be limited as much as possible, and yet within that limited sphere none but clear and correct notions would have to be given; only after the child had properly appreciated everything within it, might the sphere be gradually enlarged; care being always taken that nothing was left obscure, or half or wrongly understood. The consequence of this training would be that the child's notions of men and things would always be limited and simple in their character; but, on the other hand, they would be clear and correct, and only need to be extended, not to be rectified. The same line might be pursued on into the period of youth. This method of education would lay special stress upon the prohibition of novel reading; and the place of novels would be taken by suitable biographical literature--the life of Franklin, for instance, or Moritz' **Anton Reiser**[63].

In our early days we fancy that the leading events in our life, and the persons who are going to play an important part in it, will make their entrance to the sound of drums and trumpets; but when, in old age, we look back, we find that they all came in quite quietly, slipped in, as it were, by the side-door, almost unnoticed.

From the point of view we have been taking up until now, life may be compared to a piece of embroidery, of which, during the first half of his time, a man gets a sight of the right side, and during the second half, of the wrong. The wrong side is not so pretty as the right, but it is more instructive; it shows the way in which the threads have been worked together.

Intellectual superiority, even if it is of the highest kind, will not secure for a man a preponderating place in conversation until after he is forty years of age. For age and experience, though they can never be a substitute for intellectual talent, may far outweigh it; and even in a person of the meanest capacity, they give a certain counterpoise to the power of an extremely intellectual man, so long as the latter is young. Of course I allude here to personal superiority, not to the place a man may gain by his works.

And on passing his fortieth year, any man of the slightest power of mind--any man, that is, who has more than the sorry share of intellect with which Nature has endowed five-sixths of mankind--will hardly fail to show some trace of misanthropy. For, as is natural, he has by that time inferred other people's character from an examination of his own; with the result that he has been gradually disap-

---

63 **Translator's Note.**--Moritz was a miscellaneous writer of the last century (1757-93). His **Anton Reiser**, composed in the form of a novel, is practically an autobiography.

pointed to find that in the qualities of the head or in those of the heart--and usually in both--he reaches a level to which they do not attain; so he gladly avoids having anything more to do with them. For it may be said, in general, that every man will love or hate solitude--in other Words, his own society--just in proportion as he is worth anything in himself. Kant has some remarks upon this kind of misanthropy in his *Critique of the Faculty of Judgment*[64].

In a young man, it is a bad sign, as well from an intellectual as from a moral point of view, if he is precocious in understanding the ways of the world, and in adapting himself to its pursuits; if he at once knows how to deal with men, and enters upon life, as it were, fully prepared. It argues a vulgar nature. On the other hand, to be surprised and astonished at the way people act, and to be clumsy and cross-grained in having to do with them, indicates a character of the nobler sort.

The cheerfulness and vivacity of youth are partly due to the fact that, when we are ascending the hill of life, death is not visible: it lies down at the bottom of the other side. But once we have crossed the top of the hill, death comes in view--death--which, until then, was known to us only by hearsay. This makes our spirits droop, for at the same time we begin to feel that our vital powers are on the ebb. A grave seriousness now takes the place of that early extravagance of spirit; and the change is noticeable even in the expression of a man's face. As long as we are young, people may tell us what they please! we look upon life as endless and use our time recklessly; but the older we become, the more we practice economy. For towards the close of life, every day we live gives us the same kind of sensation as the criminal experiences at every step on his way to be tried.

From the standpoint of youth, life seems to stretch away into an endless future; from the standpoint of old age, to go back but a little way into the past; so that, at the beginning, life presents us with a picture in which the objects appear a great way off, as though we had reversed our telescope; while in the end everything seems so close. To see how short life is, a man must have grown old, that is to say, he must have lived long.

On the other hand, as the years increase, things look smaller, one and all; and Life, which had so firm and stable a base in the days of our youth, now seems nothing but a rapid flight of moments, every one of them illusory: we have come to see

---

64　*Kritik der Urtheilskraft*, Part I, Sec.29, Note ad fin.

that the whole world is vanity!

Time itself seems to go at a much slower pace when we are young; so that not only is the first quarter of life the happiest, it is also the longest of all; it leaves more memories behind it. If a man were put to it, he could tell you more out of the first quarter of his life than out of two of the remaining periods. Nay, in the spring of life, as in the spring of the year, the days reach a length that is positively tiresome; but in the autumn, whether of the year or of life, though they are short, they are more genial and uniform.

But why is it that to an old man his past life appears so short? For this reason: his memory is short; and so he fancies that his life has been short too. He no longer remembers the insignificant parts of it, and much that was unpleasant is now forgotten; how little, then, there is left! For, in general, a man's memory is as imperfect as his intellect; and he must make a practice of reflecting upon the lessons he has learned and the events he has experienced, if he does not want them both to sink gradually into the gulf of oblivion. Now, we are unaccustomed to reflect upon matters of no importance, or, as a rule, upon things that we have found disagreeable, and yet that is necessary if the memory of them is to be preserved. But the class of things that may be called insignificant is continually receiving fresh additions: much that wears an air of importance at first, gradually becomes of no consequence at all from the fact of its frequent repetition; so that in the end we actually lose count of the number of times it happens. Hence we are better able to remember the events of our early than of our later years. The longer we live, the fewer are the things that we can call important or significant enough to deserve further consideration, and by this alone can they be fixed in the memory; in other words, they are forgotten as soon as they are past. Thus it is that time runs on, leaving always fewer traces of its passage.

Further, if disagreeable things have happened to us, we do not care to ruminate upon them, least of all when they touch our vanity, as is usually the case; for few misfortunes fall upon us for which we can be held entirely blameless. So people are very ready to forget many things that are disagreeable, as well as many that are unimportant.

It is from this double cause that our memory is so short; and a man's recollection of what has happened always becomes proportionately shorter, the more things that have occupied him in life. The things we did in years gone by, the events that happened long ago, are like those objects on the coast which, to the seafarer on his outward voyage, become smaller every minute, more unrecognizable and harder to distinguish.

Again, it sometimes happens that memory and imagination will call up some long past scene as vividly as if it had occurred only yesterday; so that the event in question seems to stand very near to the present time. The reason of this is that it is impossible to call up all the intervening period in the same vivid way, as there is no one figure pervading it which can be taken in at a glance; and besides, most of the things that happened in that period are forgotten, and all that remains of it is the general knowledge that we have lived through it--a mere notion of abstract existence, not a direct vision of some particular experience. It is this that causes some single event of long ago to appear as though it took place but yesterday: the intervening time vanishes, and the whole of life looks incredibly short. Nay, there are occasional moments in old age when we can scarcely believe that we are so advanced in years, or that the long past lying behind us has had any real existence--a feeling which is mainly due to the circumstance that the present always seems fixed and immovable as we look at it. These and similar mental phenomena are ultimately to be traced to the fact that it is not our nature in itself, but only the outward presentation of it, that lies in time, and that the present is the point of contact between the world as subject and the world as object[65].

Again, why is it that in youth we can see no end to the years that seem to lie before us? Because we are obliged to find room for all the things we hope to attain in life. We cram the years so full of projects that if we were to try and carry them all out, death would come prematurely though we reached the age of Methuselah.

Another reason why life looks so long when we are young, is that we are apt to measure its length by the few years we have already lived. In those early years

---

65 *Translator's Note.*--By this remark Schopenhauer means that *will*, which, as he argues, forms the inner reality underlying all the phenomena of life and nature, is not in itself affected by time; but that, on the other hand, time is necessary for the objectification of the will, for the will as presented in the passing phenomena of the world. Time is thus definable as the condition of change, and the present time as the only point of contact between reality and appearance.

things are new to us, and so they appear important; we dwell upon them after they have happened and often call them to mind; and thus in youth life seems replete with incident, and therefore of long duration.

Sometimes we credit ourselves with a longing to be in some distant spot, whereas, in truth, we are only longing to have the time back again which we spent there--days when we were younger and fresher than we are now. In those moments Time mocks us by wearing the mask of space; and if we travel to the spot, we can see how much we have been deceived.

There are two ways of reaching a great age, both of which presuppose a sound constitution as a ***conditio sine qua non***. They may be illustrated by two lamps, one of which burns a long time with very little oil, because it has a very thin wick; and the other just as long, though it has a very thick one, because there is plenty of oil to feed it. Here, the oil is the vital energy, and the difference in the wick is the manifold way in which the vital energy is used.

Up to our thirty-sixth year, we may be compared, in respect of the way in which we use our vital energy, to people who live on the interest of their money: what they spend to-day, they have again to-morrow. But from the age of thirty-six onwards, our position is like that of the investor who begins to entrench upon his capital. At first he hardly notices any difference at all, as the greater part of his expenses is covered by the interest of his securities; and if the deficit is but slight, he pays no attention to it. But the deficit goes on increasing, until he awakes to the fact that it is becoming more serious every day: his position becomes less and less secure, and he feels himself growing poorer and poorer, while he has no expectation of this drain upon his resources coming to an end. His fall from wealth to poverty becomes faster every moment--like the fall of a solid body in space, until at last he has absolutely nothing left. A man is truly in a woeful plight if both the terms of this comparison--his vital energy and his wealth--really begin to melt away at one and the same time. It is the dread of this calamity that makes love of possession increase with age.

On the other hand, at the beginning of life, in the years before we attain majority, and for some little time afterwards--the state of our vital energy puts us on a level with those who each year lay by a part of their interest and add it to their capital: in other words, not only does their interest come in regularly, but the capital is constantly receiving additions. This happy condition of affairs is sometimes brought about--with health as with money--under the watchful care of some honest guard-ian. O happy youth, and sad old age!

Nevertheless, a man should economize his strength even when he is young. Aristotle[66] observes that amongst those who were victors at Olympia only two or three gained a prize at two different periods, once in boyhood and then again when they came to be men; and the reason of this was that the premature efforts which the training involved, so completely exhausted their powers that they failed to last on into manhood. As this is true of muscular, so it is still more true of nervous en-ergy, of which all intellectual achievements are the manifestation. Hence, those infant prodigies--*ingenia praecoda*--the fruit of a hot-house education, who sur-prise us by their cleverness as children, afterwards turn out very ordinary folk. Nay, the manner in which boys are forced into an early acquaintance with the ancient tongues may, perhaps, be to blame for the dullness and lack of judgment which distinguish so many learned persons.

I have said that almost every man's character seems to be specially suited to some one period of life, so that on reaching it the man is at his best. Some people are charming so long as they are young, and afterwards there is nothing attractive about them; others are vigorous and active in manhood, and then lose all the value they possess as they advance in years; many appear to best advantage in old age, when their character assumes a gentler tone, as becomes men who have seen the world and take life easily. This is often the case with the French.

This peculiarity must be due to the fact that the man's character has something in it akin to the qualities of youth or manhood or old age--something which ac-cords with one or another of these periods of life, or perhaps acts as a corrective to its special failings.

The mariner observes the progress he makes only by the way in which objects on the coast fade away into the distance and apparently decrease in size. In the same way a man becomes conscious that he is advancing in years when he finds that people older than himself begin to seem young to him.

It has already been remarked that the older a man becomes, the fewer are the traces left in his mind by all that he sees, does or experiences, and the cause of this

66 *Politics*.

has been explained. There is thus a sense in which it may be said that it is only in youth that a man lives with a full degree of consciousness, and that he is only half alive when he is old. As the years advance, his consciousness of what goes on about him dwindles, and the things of life hurry by without making any impression upon him, just as none is made by a work of art seen for the thousandth time. A man does what his hand finds to do, and afterwards he does not know whether he has done it or not.

As life becomes more and more unconscious, the nearer it approaches the point at which all consciousness ceases, the course of time itself seems to increase in rapidity. In childhood all the things and circumstances of life are novel; and that is sufficient to awake us to the full consciousness of existence: hence, at that age, the day seems of such immense length. The same thing happens when we are traveling: one month seems longer then than four spent at home. Still, though time seems to last longer when we are young or on a journey, the sense of novelty does not prevent it from now and then in reality hanging heavily upon our hands under both these circumstances, at any rate more than is the case when we are old or staying at home. But the intellect gradually becomes so rubbed down and blunted by long habituation to such impressions that things have a constant tendency to produce less and less impression upon us as they pass by; and this makes time seem increasingly less important, and therefore shorter in duration: the hours of the boy are longer than the days of the old man. Accordingly, time goes faster and faster the longer we live, like a ball rolling down a hill. Or, to take another example: as in a revolving disc, the further a point lies from the centre, the more rapid is its rate of progression, so it is in the wheel of life; the further you stand from the beginning, the faster time moves for you. Hence it may be said that as far as concerns the immediate sensation that time makes upon our minds, the length of any given year is in direct proportion to the number of times it will divide our whole life: for instance, at the age of fifty the year appears to us only one-tenth as long as it did at the age of five.

This variation in the rate at which time appears to move, exercises a most decided influence upon the whole nature of our existence at every period of it. First of all, it causes childhood--even though it embrace only a span of fifteen years--to seem the longest period of life, and therefore the richest in reminiscences. Next, it brings it about that a man is apt to be bored just in proportion as he is young.

Consider, for instance, that constant need of occupation--whether it is work or play--that is shown by children: if they come to an end of both work and play, a terrible feeling of boredom ensues. Even in youth people are by no means free from this tendency, and dread the hours when they have nothing to do. As manhood approaches, boredom disappears; and old men find the time too short when their days fly past them like arrows from a bow. Of course, I must be understood to speak of *men*, not of decrepit *brutes*. With this increased rapidity of time, boredom mostly passes away as we advance in life; and as the passions with all their attendant pain are then laid asleep, the burden of life is, on the whole, appreciably lighter in later years than in youth, provided, of course, that health remains. So it is that the period immediately preceding the weakness and troubles of old age, receives the name of a man's *best years*.

That may be a true appellation, in view of the comfortable feeling which those years bring; but for all that the years of youth, when our consciousness is lively and open to every sort of impression, have this privilege--that then the seeds are sown and the buds come forth; it is the springtime of the mind. Deep truths may be perceived, but can never be excogitated--that is to say, the first knowledge of them is immediate, called forth by some momentary impression. This knowledge is of such a kind as to be attainable only when the impressions are strong, lively and deep; and if we are to be acquainted with deep truths, everything depends upon a proper use of our early years. In later life, we may be better able to work upon other people,--upon the world, because our natures are then finished and rounded off, and no more a prey to fresh views; but then the world is less able to work upon us. These are the years of action and achievement; while youth is the time for forming fundamental conceptions, and laying down the ground-work of thought.

In youth it is the outward aspect of things that most engages us; while in age, thought or reflection is the predominating quality of the mind. Hence, youth is the time for poetry, and age is more inclined to philosophy. In practical affairs it is the same: a man shapes his resolutions in youth more by the impression that the outward world makes upon him; whereas, when he is old, it is thought that determines his actions. This is partly to be explained by the fact that it is only when a man is old that the results of outward observation are present in sufficient numbers to allow of their being classified according to the ideas they represent,--a process which in its turn causes those ideas to be more fully understood in all their bearings, and the exact value and amount of trust to be placed in them, fixed and determined; while at the same time he has grown accustomed to the impressions produced by the various phenomena of life, and their effects on him are no longer what they were. Contrarily, in youth, the impressions that things make, that is to say, the outward aspects of life, are so overpoweringly strong, especially in the case of people of lively and imaginative disposition, that they view the world like a picture; and their chief concern is the figure they cut in it, the appearance they present; nay, they are unaware of the extent to which this is the case. It is a quality of mind that shows itself--if in no other way--in that personal vanity, and that love of fine clothes, which distinguish young people.

There can be no doubt that the intellectual powers are most capable of enduring great and sustained efforts in youth, up to the age of thirty-five at latest; from which period their strength begins to decline, though very gradually. Still, the later years of life, and even old age itself, are not without their intellectual compensation. It is only then that a man can be said to be really rich in experience or in learning; he has then had time and opportunity enough to enable him to see and think over life from all its sides; he has been able to compare one thing with another, and to discover points of contact and connecting links, so that only then are the true relations of things rightly understood. Further, in old age there comes an increased depth in the knowledge that was acquired in youth; a man has now many more illustrations of any ideas he may have attained; things which he thought he knew when he was young, he now knows in reality. And besides, his range of knowledge is wider; and in whatever direction it extends, it is thorough, and therefore formed into a consistent and connected whole; whereas in youth knowledge is always defective and fragmentary.

A complete and adequate notion of life can never be attained by any one who does not reach old age; for it is only the old man who sees life whole and knows its natural course; it is only he who is acquainted--and this is most important--not only with its entrance, like the rest of mankind, but with its exit too; so that he alone has a full sense of its utter vanity; whilst the others never cease to labor under the false notion that everything will come right in the end.

On the other hand, there is more conceptive power in youth, and at that time

of life a man can make more out of the little that he knows. In age, judgment, pene-
tration and thoroughness predominate. Youth is the time for amassing the material
for a knowledge of the world that shall be distinctive and peculiar,--for an original
view of life, in other words, the legacy that a man of genius leaves to his fellow-
men; it is, however, only in later years that he becomes master of his material. Accordingly it will be found that, as a rule, a great writer gives his best work to the
world when he is about fifty years of age. But though the tree of knowledge must
reach its full height before it can bear fruit, the roots of it lie in youth.

Every generation, no matter how paltry its character, thinks itself much wiser
than the one immediately preceding it, let alone those that are more remote. It is
just the same with the different periods in a man's life; and yet often, in the one case
no less than in the other, it is a mistaken opinion. In the years of physical growth,
when our powers of mind and our stores of knowledge are receiving daily additions, it becomes a habit for to-day to look down with contempt upon yesterday.
The habit strikes root, and remains even after the intellectual powers have begun to
decline,--when to-day should rather look up with respect to yesterday. So it is that
we often unduly depreciate the achievements as well as the judgments of our youth.
This seems the place for making the general observation, that, although in its main
qualities a man's **intellect** or **head**, as well as his **character** or **heart**, is innate, yet
the former is by no means so unalterable in its nature as the latter. The fact is that
the intellect is subject to very many transformations, which, as a rule, do not fail to
make their actual appearance; and this is so, partly because the intellect has a deep
foundation in the physique, and partly because the material with which it deals is
given in experience. And so, from a physical point of view, we find that if a man has
any peculiar power, it first gradually increases in strength until it reaches its acme,
after which it enters upon a path of slow decadence, until it ends in imbecility. But,
on the other hand, we must not lose sight of the fact that the material which gives
employment to a man's powers and keeps them in activity,--the subject-matter of
thought and knowledge, experience, intellectual attainments, the practice of seeing
to the bottom of things, and so a perfect mental vision, form in themselves a mass
which continues to increase in size, until the time comes when weakness shows
itself, and the man's powers suddenly fail. The way in which these two distinguish-
able elements combine in the same nature,--the one absolutely unalterable, and

the other subject to change in two directions opposed to each other--explains the variety of mental attitude and the dissimilarity of value which attach to a man at different periods of life.

The same truth may be more broadly expressed by saying that the first forty years of life furnish the text, while the remaining thirty supply the commentary; and that without the commentary we are unable to understand aright the true sense and coherence of the text, together with the moral it contains and all the subtle application of which it admits.

Towards the close of life, much the same thing happens as at the end of a *bal masque*--the masks are taken off. Then you can see who the people really are, with whom you have come into contact in your passage through the world. For by the end of life characters have come out in their true light, actions have borne fruit, achievements have been rightly appreciated, and all shams have fallen to pieces. For this, Time was in every case requisite.

But the most curious fact is that it is also only towards the close of life than a man really recognizes and understands his own true self,--the aims and objects he has followed in life, more especially the kind of relation in which he has stood to other people and to the world. It will often happen that as a result of this knowledge, a man will have to assign himself a lower place than he formerly thought was his due. But there are exceptions to this rule; and it will occasionally be the case that he will take a higher position than he had before. This will be owing to the fact that he had no adequate notion of the *baseness* of the world, and that he set up a higher aim for himself than was followed by the rest of mankind.

The progress of life shows a man the stuff of which he is made.

It is customary to call youth the happy, and age the sad part of life. This would be true if it were the passions that made a man happy. Youth is swayed to and fro by them; and they give a great deal of pain and little pleasure. In age the passions cool and leave a man at rest, and then forthwith his mind takes a contemplative tone; the intellect is set free and attains the upper hand. And since, in itself, intellect is beyond the range of pain, and man feels happy just in so far as his intellect is the predominating part of him.

It need only be remembered that all pleasure is negative, and that pain is positive in its nature, in order to see that the passions can never be a source of happiness, and that age is not the less to be envied on the ground that many pleasures are denied it. For every sort of pleasure is never anything more than the quietive of some need or longing; and that pleasure should come to an end as soon as the need ceases, is no more a subject of complaint than that a man cannot go on eating after he has had his dinner, or fall asleep again after a good night's rest.

So far from youth being the happiest period of life, there is much more truth in the remark made by Plato, at the beginning of the *Republic*, that the prize should rather be given to old age, because then at last a man is freed from the animal passion which has hitherto never ceased to disquiet him. Nay, it may even be said that the countless and manifold humors which have their source in this passion, and the emotions that spring from it, produce a mild state of madness; and this lasts as long as the man is subject to the spell of the impulse--this evil spirit, as it were, of which there is no riddance--so that he never really becomes a reasonable being until the passion is extinguished.

There is no doubt that, in general, and apart from individual circumstances and particular dispositions, youth is marked by a certain melancholy and sadness, while genial sentiments attach to old age; and the reason for this is nothing but the fact that the young man is still under the service, nay, the forced labor, imposed by that evil spirit, which scarcely ever leaves him a moment to himself. To this source may be traced, directly or indirectly, almost all and every ill that befalls or menaces mankind. The old man is genial and cheerful because, after long lying in the bonds of passion, he can now move about in freedom.

Still, it should not be forgotten that, when this passion is extinguished, the true kernel of life is gone, and nothing remains but the hollow shell; or, from another point of view, life then becomes like a comedy, which, begun by real actors, is continued and brought to an end by automata dressed in their clothes.

However that may be, youth is the period of unrest, and age of repose; and from that very circumstance, the relative degree of pleasure belonging to each may be inferred. The child stretches out its little hands in the eager desire to seize all the pretty things that meet its sight, charmed by the world because all its senses are still so young and fresh. Much the same thing happens with the youth, and he displays greater energy in his quest. He, too, is charmed by all the pretty things and the many pleasing shapes that surround him; and forthwith his imagination conjures up pleasures which the world can never realize. So he is filled with an ardent desire for he knows not what delights--robbing him of all rest and making happiness impossible. But when old age is reached, all this is over and done with, partly because the blood runs cooler and the senses are no longer so easily allured; partly because experience has shown the true value of things and the futility of pleasure, whereby illusion has been gradually dispelled, and the strange fancies and prejudices which previously concealed or distorted a free and true view of the world, have been dissipated and put to flight; with the result that a man can now get a juster and clearer view, and see things as they are, and also in a measure attain more or less insight into the nullity of all things on this earth.

It is this that gives almost every old man, no matter how ordinary his faculties may be, a certain tincture of wisdom, which distinguishes him from the young. But the chief result of all this change is the peace of mind that ensues--a great element in happiness, and, in fact, the condition and essence of it. While the young man fancies that there is a vast amount of good things in the world, if he could only come at them, the old man is steeped in the truth of the Preacher's words, that ***all things are vanity***--knowing that, however gilded the shell, the nut is hollow.

In these later years, and not before, a man comes to a true appreciation of Horace's maxim: ***Nil admirari.*** He is directly and sincerely convinced of the vanity of everything and that all the glories of the world are as nothing: his illusions are gone. He is no more beset with the idea that there is any particular amount of happiness anywhere, in the palace or in the cottage, any more than he himself enjoys when he is free from bodily or mental pain. The worldly distinctions of great and small, high and low, exist for him no longer; and in this blissful state of mind the old man may look down with a smile upon all false notions. He is completely undeceived, and knows that whatever may be done to adorn human life and deck it out in finery, its paltry character will soon show through the glitter of its surroundings; and that, paint and be jewel it as one may, it remains everywhere much the same,--an existence which has no true value except in freedom from pain, and is never to be estimated by the presence of pleasure, let alone, then, of display[67].

Disillusion is the chief characteristic of old age; for by that time the fictions are gone which gave life its charm and spurred on the mind to activity; the splendors

---

67 Cf. Horace, ***Epist***. I. 12, I-4.

of the world have been proved null and vain; its pomp, grandeur and magnificence are faded. A man has then found out that behind most of the things he wants, and most of the pleasures he longs for, there is very little after all; and so he comes by degrees to see that our existence is all empty and void. It is only when he is seventy years old that he quite understands the first words of the Preacher; and this again explains why it is that old men are sometimes fretful and morose.

It is often said that the common lot of old age is disease and weariness of life. Disease is by no means essential to old age; especially where a really long span of years is to be attained; for as life goes on, the conditions of health and disorder tend to increase--*crescente vita, crescit sanitas et morbus*. And as far as weariness or boredom is concerned, I have stated above why old age is even less exposed to that form of evil than youth. Nor is boredom by any means to be taken as a necessary accompaniment of that solitude, which, for reasons that do not require to be explained, old age certainly cannot escape; it is rather the fate that awaits those who have never known any other pleasures but the gratification of the senses and the delights of society--who have left their minds unenlightened and their faculties unused. It is quite true that the intellectual faculties decline with the approach of old age; but where they were originally strong, there will always be enough left to combat the onslaught of boredom. And then again, as I have said, experience, knowledge, reflection, and skill in dealing with men, combine to give an old man an increasingly accurate insight into the ways of the world; his judgment becomes keen and he attains a coherent view of life: his mental vision embraces a wider range. Constantly finding new uses for his stores of knowledge and adding to them at every opportunity, he maintains uninterrupted that inward process of self-education, which gives employment and satisfaction to the mind, and thus forms the due reward of all its efforts.

All this serves in some measure as a compensation for decreased intellectual power. And besides, Time, as I have remarked, seems to go much more quickly when we are advanced in years; and this is in itself a preventive of boredom. There is no great harm in the fact that a man's bodily strength decreases in old age, unless, indeed, he requires it to make a living. To be poor when one is old, is a great misfortune. If a man is secure from that, and retains his health, old age may be a very passable time of life. Its chief necessity is to be comfortable and well off; and, in consequence, money is then prized more than ever, because it is a substitute for failing strength. Deserted by Venus, the old man likes to turn to Bacchus to make him merry. In the place of wanting to see things, to travel and learn, comes the desire to speak and teach. It is a piece of good fortune if the old man retains some of his love of study or of music or of the theatre,--if, in general, he is still somewhat susceptible to the things about him; as is, indeed, the case with some people to a very late age. At that time of life, ***what a man has in himself*** is of greater advantage to him that ever it was before.

There can be no doubt that most people who have never been anything but dull and stupid, become more and more of automata as they grow old. They have always thought, said and done the same things as their neighbors; and nothing that happens now can change their disposition, or make them act otherwise. To talk to old people of this kind is like writing on the sand; if you produce any impression at all, it is gone almost immediately; old age is here nothing but the ***caput mortuum*** of life--all that is essential to manhood is gone. There are cases in which nature supplies a third set of teeth in old age, thereby apparently demonstrating the fact that that period of life is a second childhood.

It is certainly a very melancholy thing that all a man's faculties tend to waste away as he grows old, and at a rate that increases in rapidity: but still, this is a necessary, nay, a beneficial arrangement, as otherwise death, for which it is a preparation, would be too hard to bear. So the greatest boon that follows the attainment of extreme old age is ***euthanasia***,--an easy death, not ushered in by disease, and free from all pain and struggle[68]. For let a man live as long as he may, he is never conscious of any moment but the present, one and indivisible; and in those late years the mind loses more every day by sheer forgetfulness than ever it gains anew.

The main difference between youth and age will always be that youth looks forward to life, and old age to death; and that while the one has a short past and a long future before it, the case is just the opposite with the other. It is quite true that when a man is old, to die is the only thing that awaits him; while if he is young, he may expect to live; and the question arises which of the two fates is the more hazardous, and if life is not a matter which, on the whole, it is better to have be-

68 See ***Die Welt als Wille und Vorstellung***, Bk. II. ch. 41, for a further description of this happy end to life.

hind one than before? Does not the Preacher say: the day of death [is better] than the day of one's birth[69]. It is certainly a rash thing to wish for long life[70]; for as the Spanish proverb has it, it means to see much evil,--*Quien larga vida vive mucho mal vide*.

A man's individual career is not, as Astrology wishes to make out, to be predicted from observation of the planets; but the course of human life in general, as far as the various periods of it are concerned, may be likened to the succession of the planets: so that we may be said to pass under the influence of each one of them

69 Ecclesiastes vii. 1.

70 The life of man cannot, strictly speaking, be called either *long* or *short*, since it is the ultimate standard by which duration of time in regard to all other things is measured.

In one of the Vedic Upanishads (Oupnekhat, II.) *the natural length* of human life is put down at one hundred years. And I believe this to be right. I have observed, as a matter of fact, that it is only people who exceed the age of ninety who attain *euthanasia*,--who die, that is to say, of no disease, apoplexy or convulsion, and pass away without agony of any sort; nay, who sometimes even show no pallor, but expire generally in a sitting attitude, and often after a meal,--or, I may say, simply cease to live rather than die. To come to one's end before the age of ninety, means to die of disease, in other words, prematurely.

Now the Old Testament (Psalms xc. 10) puts the limit of human life at seventy, and if it is very long, at eighty years; and what is more noticeable still, Herodotus (i. 32 and iii. 22) says the same thing. But this is wrong; and the error is due simply to a rough and superficial estimate of the results of daily experience. For if the natural length of life were from seventy to eighty years, people would die, about that time, of mere old age. Now this is certainly not the case. If they die then, they die, like younger people, *of disease*; and disease is something abnormal. Therefore it is not natural to die at that age. It is only when they are between ninety and a hundred that people die of old age; die, I mean, without suffering from any disease, or showing any special signs of their condition, such as a struggle, death-rattle, convulsion, pallor,--the absence of all which constitutes *euthanasia*. The natural length of human life is a hundred years; and in assigning that limit the Upanishads are right once more.

in turn.

At ten, *Mercury* is in the ascendant; and at that age, a youth, like this planet, is characterized by extreme mobility within a narrow sphere, where trifles have a great effect upon him; but under the guidance of so crafty and eloquent a god, he easily makes great progress. *Venus* begins her sway during his twentieth year, and then a man is wholly given up to the love of women. At thirty, *Mars* comes to the front, and he is now all energy and strength,--daring, pugnacious and arrogant.

When a man reaches the age of forty, he is under the rule of the four *Asteroids*; that is to say, his life has gained something in extension. He is frugal; in other words, by the help of *Ceres*, he favors what is useful; he has his own hearth, by the influence of *Vesta*; *Pallas* has taught him that which is necessary for him to know; and his wife--his *Juno*--rules as the mistress of his house.

But at the age of fifty, *Jupiter* is the dominant influence. At that period a man has outlived most of his contemporaries, and he can feel himself superior to the generation about him. He is still in the full enjoyment of his strength, and rich in experience and knowledge; and if he has any power and position of his own, he is endowed with authority over all who stand in his immediate surroundings. He is no more inclined to receive orders from others; he wants to take command himself. The work most suitable to him now is to guide and rule within his own sphere. This is the point where Jupiter culminates, and where the man of fifty years is at his best.

Then comes *Saturn*, at about the age of sixty, a weight as of *lead*, dull and slow:--

>*But old folks, many feign as they were dead;*
>*Unwieldy, slow, heavy and pale as lead.* Last of all, *Uranus*; or, as the saying is, a man goes to heaven.

I cannot find a place for *Neptune*, as this planet has been very thoughtlessly named; because I may not call it as it should be called--*Eros*. Otherwise I should point out how Beginning and End meet together, and how closely and intimately Eros is connected with Death: how Orcus, or Amenthes, as the Egyptians called him, is not only the receiver but the giver of all things--[Greek: lambanon kai did-ous]. Death is the great reservoir of Life. Everything comes from Orcus; everything that is alive now was once there. Could we but understand the great trick by which that is done, all would be clear!

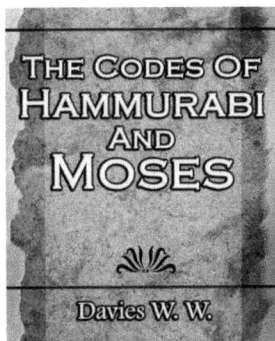

The Codes Of Hammurabi And Moses
W. W. Davies

The discovery of the Hammurabi Code is one of the greatest achievements of archaeology, and is of paramount interest, not only to the student of the Bible, but also to all those interested in ancient history...

Religion   **ISBN:** *1-59462-338-4*   **Pages:**132

QTY

MSRP $12.95

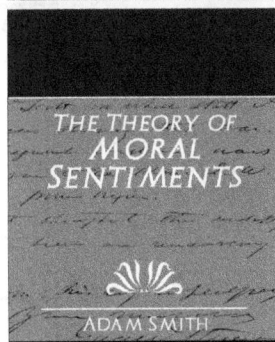

The Theory of Moral Sentiments
Adam Smith

This work from 1749. contains original theories of conscience amd moral judgment and it is the foundation for systemof morals.

Philosophy **ISBN:** *1-59462-777-0*   **Pages:**536

QTY

MSRP $19.95

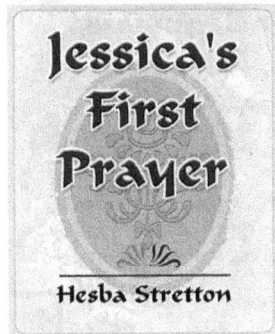

Jessica's First Prayer
Hesba Stretton

In a screened and secluded corner of one of the many railway-bridges which span the streets of London there could be seen a few years ago, from five o'clock every morning until half past eight, a tidily set-out coffee-stall, consisting of a trestle and board, upon which stood two large tin cans, with a small fire of charcoal burning under each so as to keep the coffee boiling during the early hours of the morning when the work-people were thronging into the city on their way to their daily toil...

QTY

Pages:84

Childrens   **ISBN:** *1-59462-373-2*   *MSRP $9.95*

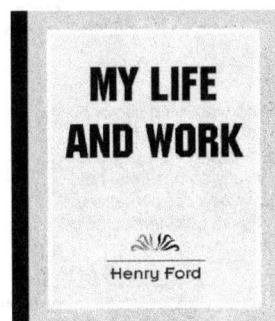

My Life and Work
Henry Ford

QTY

Henry Ford revolutionized the world with his implementation of mass production for the Model T automobile. Gain valuable business insight into his life and work with his own auto-biography... "We have only started on our development of our country we have not as yet, with all our talk of wonderful progress, done more than scratch the surface. The progress has been wonderful enough but..."

Pages:300

Biographies/   **ISBN:** *1-59462-198-5*   *MSRP $21.95*

The Art of Cross-Examination
Francis Wellman

QTY

I presume it is the experience of every author, after his first book is published upon an important subject, to be almost overwhelmed with a wealth of ideas and illustrations which could readily have been included in his book, and which to his own mind, at least, seem to make a second edition inevitable. Such certainly was the case with me; and when the first edition had reached its sixth impression in five months, I rejoiced to learn that it seemed to my publishers that the book had met with a sufficiently favorable reception to justify a second and considerably enlarged edition. ..

Pages:412

Reference ISBN: *1-59462-647-2*

MSRP $19.95

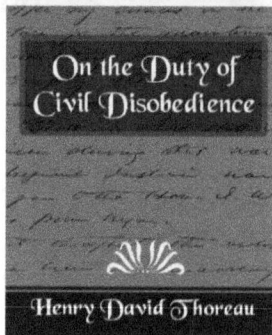

On the Duty of Civil Disobedience
Henry David Thoreau

QTY

Thoreau wrote his famous essay, On the Duty of Civil Disobedience, as a protest against an unjust but popular war and the immoral but popular institution of slave-owning. He did more than write—he declined to pay his taxes, and was hauled off to gaol in consequence. Who can say how much this refusal of his hastened the end of the war and of slavery ?

Law ISBN: *1-59462-747-9*

Pages:48

MSRP $7.45

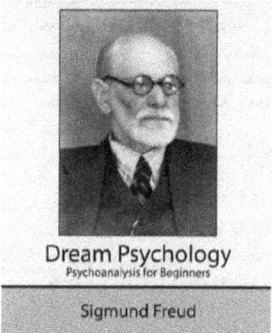

Dream Psychology Psychoanalysis for Beginners
Sigmund Freud

QTY

Sigmund Freud, born Sigismund Schlomo Freud (May 6, 1856 - September 23, 1939), was a Jewish-Austrian neurologist and psychiatrist who co-founded the psychoanalytic school of psychology. Freud is best known for his theories of the unconscious mind, especially involving the mechanism of repression; his redefinition of sexual desire as mobile and directed towards a wide variety of objects; and his therapeutic techniques, especially his understanding of transference in the therapeutic relationship and the presumed value of dreams as sources of insight into unconscious desires.

Pages:196

Psychology ISBN: *1-59462-905-6*

MSRP $15.45

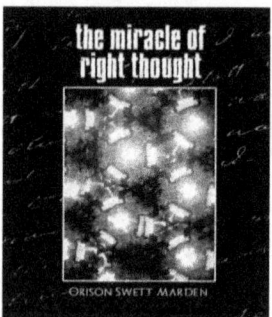

The Miracle of Right Thought
Orison Swett Marden

QTY

Believe with all of your heart that you will do what you were made to do. When the mind has once formed the habit of holding cheerful, happy, prosperous pictures, it will not be easy to form the opposite habit. It does not matter how improbable or how far away this realization may see, or how dark the prospects may be, if we visualize them as best we can, as vividly as possible, hold tenaciously to them and vigorously struggle to attain them, they will gradually become actualized, realized in the life. But a desire, a longing without endeavor, a yearning abandoned or held indifferently will vanish without realization.

Pages:360

Self Help ISBN: *1-59462-644-8*

MSRP $25.45

QTY

The Rosicrucian Cosmo-Conception Mystic Christianity *by Max Heindel*   ISBN: *1-59462-188-8* **$38.95**
The Rosicrucian Cosmo-conception is not dogmatic, neither does it appeal to any other authority than the reason of the student. It is: not controversial, but is: sent forth in the, hope that it may help to clear...   New Age/Religion Pages 646

Abandonment To Divine Providence *by Jean-Pierre de Caussade*   ISBN: *1-59462-228-0* **$25.95**
"The Rev. Jean Pierre de Caussade was one of the most remarkable spiritual writers of the Society of Jesus in France in the 18th Century. His death took place at Toulouse in 1751. His works have gone through many editions and have been republished...   Inspirational/Religion Pages 400

Mental Chemistry *by Charles Haanel*   ISBN: *1-59462-192-6* **$23.95**
Mental Chemistry allows the change of material conditions by combining and appropriately utilizing the power of the mind. Much like applied chemistry creates something new and unique out of careful combinations of chemicals the mastery of mental chemistry...   New Age Pages 354

The Letters of Robert Browning and Elizabeth Barret Barrett 1845-1846 vol II   ISBN: *1-59462-193-4* **$35.95**
by Robert Browning and *Elizabeth Barrett*   Biographies Pages 596

Gleanings In Genesis (volume I) *by Arthur W. Pink*   ISBN: *1-59462-130-6* **$27.45**
Appropriately has Genesis been termed "the seed plot of the Bible" for in it we have, in germ form, almost all of the great doctrines which are afterwards fully developed in the books of Scripture which follow...   Religion/Inspirational Pages 420

The Master Key *by L. W. de Laurence*   ISBN: *1-59462-001-6* **$30.95**
In no branch of human knowledge has there been a more lively increase of the spirit of research during the past few years than in the study of Psychology, Concentration and Mental Discipline. The requests for authentic lessons in Thought Control, Mental Discipline and...   New Age/Business Pages 422

The Lesser Key Of Solomon Goetia *by L. W. de Laurence*   ISBN: *1-59462-092-X* **$9.95**
This translation of the first book of the "Lernegton" which is now for the first time made accessible to students of Talismanic Magic was done, after careful collation and edition, from numerous Ancient Manuscripts in Hebrew, Latin, and French...   New Age/Occult Pages 92

Rubaiyat Of Omar Khayyam *by Edward Fitzgerald*   ISBN:*1-59462-332-5* **$13.95**
Edward Fitzgerald, whom the world has already learned, in spite of his own efforts to remain within the shadow of anonymity, to look upon as one of the rarest poets of the century, was born at Bredfield, in Suffolk, on the 31st of March, 1809. He was the third son of John Purcell...   Music Pages 172

Ancient Law *by Henry Maine*   ISBN: *1-59462-128-4* **$29.95**
The chief object of the following pages is to indicate some of the earliest ideas of mankind, as they are reflected in Ancient Law, and to point out the relation of those ideas to modern thought.   Religion/History Pages 452

Far-Away Stories *by William J. Locke*   ISBN: *1-59462-129-2* **$19.45**
"Good wine needs no bush, but a collection of mixed vintages does. And this book is just such a collection. Some of the stories I do not want to remain buried for ever in the museum files of dead magazine-numbers an author's not unpardonable vanity..."   Fiction Pages 272

Life of David Crockett *by David Crockett*   ISBN: *1-59462-250-7* **$27.45**
"Colonel David Crockett was one of the most remarkable men of the times in which he lived. Born in humble life, but gifted with a strong will, an indomitable courage, and unremitting perseverance...   Biographies/New Age Pages 424

Lip-Reading *by Edward Nitchie*   ISBN: *1-59462-206-X* **$25.95**
Edward B. Nitchie, founder of the New York School for the Hard of Hearing, now the Nitchie School of Lip-Reading, Inc, wrote "LIP-READING Principles and Practice". The development and perfecting of this meritorious work on lip-reading was an undertaking...   How-to Pages 400

A Handbook of Suggestive Therapeutics, Applied Hypnotism, Psychic Science   ISBN: *1-59462-214-0* **$24.95**
by Henry Munro   Health/New Age/Health/Self-help Pages 376

A Doll's House: and Two Other Plays *by Henrik Ibsen*   ISBN: *1-59462-112-8* **$19.95**
Henrik Ibsen created this classic when in revolutionary 1848 Rome. Introducing some striking concepts in playwriting for the realist genre, this play has been studied the world over.   Fiction/Classics/Plays 308

The Light of Asia *by sir Edwin Arnold*   ISBN: *1-59462-204-3* **$13.95**
In this poetic masterpiece, Edwin Arnold describes the life and teachings of Buddha. The man who was to become known as Buddha to the world was born as Prince Gautama of India but he rejected the worldly riches and abandoned the reigns of power when...   Religion/History/Biographies Pages 170

The Complete Works of Guy de Maupassant *by Guy de Maupassant*   ISBN: *1-59462-157-8* **$16.95**
"For days and days, nights and nights, I had dreamed of that first kiss which was to consecrate our engagement, and I knew not on what spot I should put my lips..."   Fiction/Classics Pages 240

The Art of Cross-Examination *by Francis L. Wellman*   ISBN: *1-59462-309-0* **$26.95**
Written by a renowned trial lawyer, Wellman imparts his experience and uses case studies to explain how to use psychology to extract desired information through questioning.   How-to/Science/Reference Pages 408

Answered or Unanswered? *by Louisa Vaughan*   ISBN: *1-59462-248-5* **$10.95**
Miracles of Faith in China   Religion Pages 112

The Edinburgh Lectures on Mental Science (1909) *by Thomas*   ISBN: *1-59462-008-3* **$11.95**
This book contains the substance of a course of lectures recently given by the writer in the Queen Street Hall, Edinburgh. Its purpose is to indicate the Natural Principles governing the relation between Mental Action and Material Conditions...   New Age/Psychology Pages 148

Ayesha *by H. Rider Haggard*   ISBN: *1-59462-301-5* **$24.95**
Verily and indeed it is the unexpected that happens! Probably if there was one person upon the earth from whom the Editor of this, and of a certain previous history, did not expect to hear again...   Classics Pages 380

Ayala's Angel *by Anthony Trollope*   ISBN: *1-59462-352-X* **$29.95**
The two girls were both pretty, but Lucy who was twenty-one who supposed to be simple and comparatively unattractive, whereas Ayala was credited, as her Bombwhat romantic name might show, with poetic charm and a taste for romance. Ayala when her father died was nineteen...   Fiction Pages 484

The American Commonwealth *by James Bryce*   ISBN: *1-59462-286-8* **$34.45**
An interpretation of American democratic political theory. It examines political mechanics and society from the perspective of Scotsman James Bryce   Politics Pages 572

Stories of the Pilgrims *by Margaret P. Pumphrey*   ISBN: *1-59462-116-0* **$17.95**
This book explores pilgrims religious oppression in England as well as their escape to Holland and eventual crossing to America on the Mayflower, and their early days in New England...   History Pages 268

QTY

The Fasting Cure *by Sinclair Upton*   ISBN: *1-59462-222-1* **$13.95**
In the Cosmopolitan Magazine for May, 1910, and in the Contemporary Review (London) for April, 1910, I published an article dealing with my experi-
ences in fasting. I have written a great many magazine articles, but never one which attracted so much attention... New Age/Self Help/Health Pages 164

Hebrew Astrology *by Sepharial*   ISBN: *1-59462-308-2* **$13.45**
In these days of advanced thinking it is a matter of common observation that we have left many of the old landmarks behind and that we are now pressing
forward to greater heights and to a wider horizon than that which represented the mind-content of our progenitors... Astrology Pages 144

Thought Vibration or The Law of Attraction in the Thought World   ISBN: *1-59462-127-6* **$12.95**

by William Walker Atkinson   Psychology/Religion Pages 144

Optimism *by Helen Keller*   ISBN: *1-59462-108-X* **$15.95**
Helen Keller was blind, deaf, and mute since 19 months old, yet famously learned how to overcome these handicaps, communicate with the world, and
spread her lectures promoting optimism. An inspiring read for everyone... Biographies/Inspirational Pages 84

Sara Crewe *by Frances Burnett*   ISBN: *1-59462-360-0* **$9.45**
In the first place, Miss Minchin lived in London. Her home was a large, dull, tall one, in a large, dull square, where all the houses were alike, and all the
sparrows were alike, and where all the door-knockers made the same heavy sound... Childrens/Classic Pages 88

The Autobiography of Benjamin Franklin *by Benjamin Franklin*   ISBN: *1-59462-135-7* **$24.95**
The Autobiography of Benjamin Franklin has probably been more extensively read than any other American historical work, and no other book of its kind
has had such ups and downs of fortune. Franklin lived for many years in England, where he was agent... Biographies/History Pages 332

Name	
Email	
Telephone	
Address	
City, State ZIP	

☐ **Credit Card**   ☐ **Check / Money Order**

Credit Card Number	
Expiration Date	
Signature	

Please Mail to: Book Jungle
                              PO Box 2226
                              Champaign, IL 61825
or Fax to: 630-214-0564

ORDERING INFORMATION
web*: www.bookjungle.com*
email*: sales@bookjungle.com*
fax*: 630-214-0564*
mail*: Book Jungle PO Box 2226 Champaign, IL 61825*
or PayPal *to sales@bookjungle.com*

Please contact us for bulk discounts

DIRECT-ORDER TERMS

**20% Discount if You Order
Two or More Books**
Free Domestic Shipping!
Accepted: Master Card, Visa,
Discover, American Express